THE BOOK OF
SOUND THERAPY

Heal yourself with music and voice

OLIVEA DEWHURST-MADDOCK

A GAIA ORIGINAL

A Fireside Book
Published by Simon & Schuster Inc.
New York   London   Toronto   Sydney   Tokyo   Singapore

A GAIA ORIGINAL

Conceived by Joss Pearson

Editorial	Steve Parker
Design	Ellen Moorcraft
Illustration	Sally Downes
	Debbie Hinks
Direction	Joss Pearson
	Patrick Nugent
	Eleanor Lines

Note on the exercises
If you have any injury or chronic illness, consult your physician before attempting the exercises in this book.

FIRESIDE
Simon & Schuster Building
Rockefeller Center
1230 Avenue of the Americas
New York, New York 10020

Printed and bound in Singapore by Imago

10 9 8 7 6 5 4 3 2 1

Library of Congress Cataloging-in-Publication Data
Dewhurst-Maddock, Olivea.
  Sound therapy / Olivea Dewhurst-Maddock.
    p. cm.
  "A Fireside Book"
  Includes bibliographical references.
  ISBN 0-671-78639-3
  1. Sound—therapeutic use. 2. Voice—therapeutic use. I. Title.
  RZ999.D49 1993
  615.8'51—dc20   92-13804
                    CIP

This book is dedicated to
JACK

FOREWORD

This book represents another breakthrough in vital healing. It is thrilling. The New Age adventure leads us into fields of light and greater understanding. Olivea Dewhurst-Maddock, rich in experience and training in creative music and song, has demonstrated a form of therapy that may well have profound implications. As musician and singer, she offers a practical introduction to using the voice and instrumental music for sound therapy. Her book gives us a general understanding of this form of vibrational healing, as a therapeutic approach unlike most other systems of healing. She is, indeed, to be congratulated on this achievement. Her thinking and experience should inspire many people working in the creative fields of sound, music, and the healing arts.

George Trevelyan

Sir George Trevelyan

Olivea Dewhurst-Maddock has studied the voice, sound, and music since the age of three. She qualified as a Licenciate of London's Royal Academy of Music and gained a teacher's diploma in singing from the Royal College of Music. After five years with the Sadler's Wells Opera, followed by travel and work in Europe, Olivea taught vocal studies at many colleges of education. Continuing her interest in the meanings behind music, she has attended and taught at many contemporary schools of New Age philosophy and healing. She travels widely, works as a music therapist and counsellor, and teaches therapeutic breathing, relaxation, and meditation.

CONTENTS

INTRODUCTION

Sound is created as the vibratory motion of particles and objects. The vibrations that produce sound represent an energy that is found throughout nature, not only within ourselves and our world, but far beyond, into the realms of moons, stars, and the Universe. Due to the limitations of human physiology, our own ears can detect only a tiny fraction of this vast vibratory spectrum. On the cosmic scale, sound is a universal, unseen power, able to bring about profound changes on many levels—physical, emotional, and spiritual. This book explains how you can harness and direct the power of sound—as the vibratory energies of your own voice, and as sounds from the world around, making them resonate through your body and mind, to heal and cure.

Music is a special type of sound. It not only pleases our ears. The patterns of its vibratory motions encapsulate a system of rhythms, relationships, proportions, and harmonies that exist throughout the natural and the human-made world—from the movements of the planets around the Sun, to the growth of cells and plants, to the sacred numbers and ratios of ancient beliefs and religions, to art, architecture, and mathematics. Music is a universal human language: of initiation in rites of passage, as a guide through the labyrinths of expanding consciousness, and as a route to deep healing and spiritual fulfilment.

People have used sounds, particularly musical sounds, naturally and therapeutically through the centuries. The origins of healing by sound and music can be traced into prehistory and beyond, into the realms of myth, religion, and the memory of the soul.

The Classical era

In ancient Egypt, the hieroglyph for music was also that for joy and wellbeing. The Vedic-Sanskrit scholars of ancient India, and the philosophers of the school of Pythagoras in Classical Greece, regarded all physical forms as manifestations of music; as we shall see, the relative proportions of musical sounds parallel the physical proportions of natural and architectural shapes. These ancient doctrines held that

Sound and music have enormous potential to bring together the hearts and minds of millions, for common causes. The success of musical fund-raising events, such as helping to Feed the World, demonstrates the powerful uniting effects of shared music.

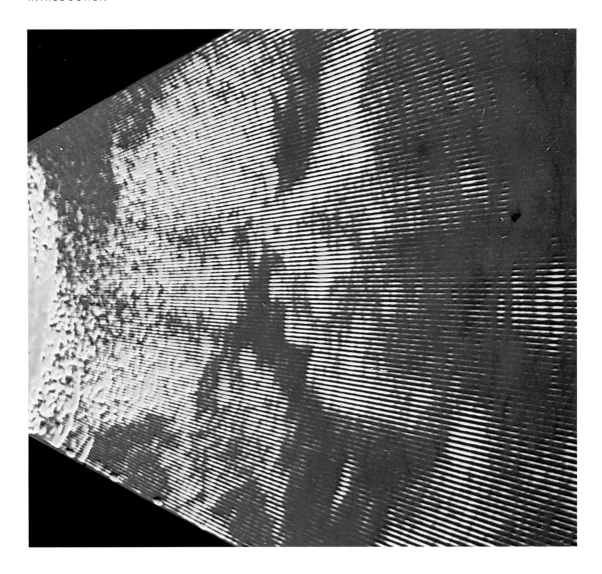

life and health depended upon a continuum of ratios and harmonic relationships, from within the mind and through the body, out to society and the natural world. The same ratios and harmonics were manifested as sound and music. Correctly applied, sound could bring about cures by restoring the musical integrity of body and soul. Ancient prescriptions often included rhythmic singing and chanting, from a traditional selection of sacred melodic sequences.

The learned peoples of ancient cultures perceived earthly music as an echo or resonance of cosmic music, obeying the same divine laws. If these earthly sounds reflected the divine laws, they had the power to ease pain and suffering, and promote health and healing. Cosmology and musical theory

Seeing with sound: a computer-enhanced scan of a baby's face (looking towards the left), two months before birth. The image is made by detecting the echoes of ultrasound, sounds that are too high-pitched for human ears (see page 29).

were therefore developed on parallel principles, which governed the design and making of musical instruments, composing and performing, and the attitude of the listener. Humanity, rightly tuned, could sing in consort with the stars in this quest for universal harmony.

Musical reverence

The power of music to evoke emotional response has been a recurring theme of poetic celebration, and the life-blood of performance. Music can bypass the mind's logical and analytical filters, to make direct contact with profound feelings and passions deep in the memory and imagination. This, in turn, produces physical reactions.

Physical effects can be induced in other ways. Energies, including sound energy, are morally neutral. That is, they can be used for good or ill. Sound is a potent force; when abused it can irritate, disorientate, injure, even kill. Reverence for life, and a sense of moral responsibility, are imperative for the appropriate use of sonic energies. This sense of responsibility was required by students of Classical philosophy in ancient Greece and Rome, where healing music was carefully chosen to ensure health, purity, and a stable character.

Sound's healing powers

Healing mantras, chants, and incantations have very ancient and obscure origins. Yet their achievements litter history. The knowledge of rhythms, sounds, and words of power have survived centuries of materialism, and they remain a living heritage for the future.

Egyptian medical papyri from 2,600 years ago refer to incantations as cures for infertility, rheumatic pain, and insect bites. In about 324 BC, the music of the lyre restored Alexander the Great to sanity. The Old Testament records that David played his harp and lifted King Saul's depression. The Essenes and Therapeutai used sacred words for healing. And in Hellenistic culture, flute-playing eased the pain of sciatica and gout.

Knowledge of sounds, rhythms, and chants was an essential ingredient in the healing powers of the shaman, the medicine man or woman, and the druidic priest-doctors of Celtic cultures. The theme of music as a metaphor for divine order and loveliness pervades the mystical literature of Judaism, Christianity, Islam, and Gnosticism.

Renaissance healing

The great scholars and teachers of medieval and Renaissance times recognized music's central importance in the understanding of the Universe and humanity. Among these polymaths were healers and doctors. The physician Thomas Campian, remembered for his exquisite lyrics and vocal compositions, practised psychological healing of depression and similar problems through his songs, in the reign of Elizabeth I. In Jacobean England, Thomas Cogan and Richard Brown treated their patients with music.

Great composers detected the links between sound, music, and health. George Frederick Handel reportedly stated that he did not wish to amuse his audiences by his compositions—he wished "to make them better". Farinelli, the eighteenth century's pre-eminent male opera singer, cured Spain's Philip V of a chronic sickness by repeatedly singing the king's favourite aria. Martinus, another vocalist of the period, described how his performances reduced high fever in members of his audience. He reasoned that the virtues of music, transmitted by the singer through the air, entered the patient's body to restore natural vigour and wellbeing.

Measuring the effects of sound

The nineteenth century saw scientific research into the physiological effects of music, by measuring its effects on respiration, heart rate, circulation, and blood pressure. As a result of this research, selected musical sequences have successfully relieved specific kinds of pain. Gradually, the value of sound and music as therapeutic techniques won a measure of recognition, especially in areas of mental health, psychological rehabilitation, and occupational therapy.

Scientific studies have reinforced the notion that resonance is basic to healing with sound and music. The acoustic principle of resonance (explained more fully in Chapter One) applies not only to musical instruments, but also to the human body. As the sound waves enter the body, sympathetic vibrations occur in its living cells, which help to restore and reinforce healthy organization. The high water content of the body's tissues helps to conduct sound, and the overall effect is likened to a deep massage at the atomic and molecular level.

The human being is therefore likened to a very complex, unique, and finely-tuned musical instrument. Every atom, molecule, cell, tissue, and organ of the body continually broadcasts the frequencies of physical, emotional, mental, and spiritual life. The human voice is an indicator of its body's health on all these levels of existence. It establishes a relationship between the individual and the wondrous network of vibrations that is the cosmos.

Toward a comprehensive vision

No scientific or spiritual progress is a smooth, uninterrupted ascent. There are the inevitable false trails and disappointments. Progress in the holistic view of music is occasionally weakened by elitism, and degraded by commercial banality. But it is never lost. The mystical river of sacred sound flows underground, and reappears wherever ageless wisdom is cherished. To build upon our direct experiences, and rediscover meaning in life, is the challenge. Prescribed wisdom is not enough. Second-hand persuasions leave us unsatisfied. We aspire to a comprehensive vision that can link the peaks of spiritual elevation with the dust and turmoil of everyday life. Sound and music can turn the vision into reality.

Human consciousness embraces an intuitive conviction that life is sacred, which is powerful enough to outweigh the dangers of self-destruction that haunt our age. Oblivion is not inevitable. We can choose peace, shared abundance, and positive health. This book offers a way to enter into the processes of personal and planetary harmonization.

Music is silence and sound, dancing together in space.
The heavens are music, the earth is music.
Called into being, we listen.
Living resonances of the word, we sing.
Embracing in silence and sound, together in endless song, is harmony.
Listen with love. Awaken to music.
Sounding the truth, together, is healing.

Sound is an integral part of life. From the earliest times, humans have used sounds to provide information about the world around them, and to communicate with each other. During your earliest days, as an unborn baby, there were sounds of your mother's heartbeat, and a muffled introduction to the outside world.

You live in a world of sounds. Sounds heard and unheard; sounds musical and chaotic; sounds strange and familiar; sounds stressful and pleasing; sounds that shatter, and sounds that heal. This chapter explores the science of those sounds; how they are produced, transmitted, and aurally perceived; and how the relationships, proportions, and harmonies of musical sounds share qualities that are universal, and reflect patterns that exist throughout nature. Knowing some of this scientific background will help to deepen your understanding of how sounds are used therapeutically.

Sound is motion. More specifically, sound is vibrational motion—produced when objects move to and fro, or oscillate, in the manner of a swinging pendulum bob. At a fundamental level, sound is the motion of atoms and molecules. The sounds coming from objects—from a mosquito's tiny wings to a gale-thrashed tree—originate from the movement of the millions of atoms and molecules that make up such objects. In fact, sounds come from objects as small as an atom, or as large as a planet.

"There is in souls a sympathy with sounds,
And as the mind is pitch'd the ear is pleased,
With melting airs, or martial, brisk or grave,
Some chord in unison with what we hear,
Is touch'd within us, and the heart replies."

William Cowper

NATURE OF SOUND EXERCISE

Examine a sound-producing object such as a guitar string, loudspeaker cone, or tuning fork. You may be able to see the to-and-fro vibrations that create the sound, and how they eventually die away as the sound decays. If the vibrations happen so fast that your eye cannot follow them, and the movement looks just like a blur, gently touch the object. Fingertips can feel vibrations that are too tiny or fast for the eye to see. Your fingers can probably feel the vibrations, but they will also damp them down, so that the sound dies away more quickly.

Dinka musicians from Sudan, Africa, play a variety of percussion and wind instruments. Rhythmic percussion and the involvement of the breath produce very personal sounds that may be used therapeutically, as well as for communication and celebration.

Sound and energy

In classical science, energy is defined as the capacity to do work—to "make things happen". A moving object can make things happen, by virtue of the energy represented by its motion. A flowing river has the energy to turn huge turbine blades connected to electricity generators. In this way, the energy of moving water is converted into electrical energy. This type of energy, possessed by objects or substances on the move, is known as kinetic energy.

Sound exists as a result of the vibrational movements of objects. So it, too, is a form of kinetic energy. This energy can be chaotic or ordered, weak or powerful. All the sound energy produced by the cheering, clapping crowd at a major sporting event would, if converted to heat energy, barely

As the tuning fork's prongs vibrate, they produce regions of high and low pressure in the air immediately adjacent to them. These regions spread outward, as sound waves that "ripple" through the air (see page 20).

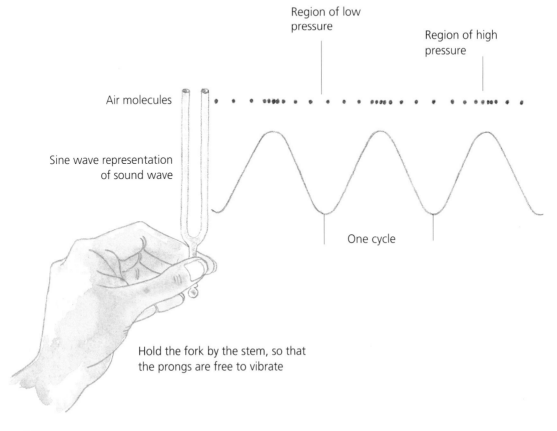

Region of low pressure

Region of high pressure

Air molecules

Sine wave representation of sound wave

One cycle

Hold the fork by the stem, so that the prongs are free to vibrate

boil enough water for a cup of coffee. In modern medicine a powerful, high-pitched beam of sound can be so precisely focused that it can vibrate and shatter mineralized stones in the kidneys or gall-bladder. It is the nature of sound at this energetic level that accounts for the wide range of its effects on body and mind.

Cycles, frequency, and pitch

High-pitched sounds have more oscillations, or cycles, per second than low-pitched ones. A high-pitched sound is represented by waves that are squashed closer together than in low-pitched sounds. This means the wavelengths of high-pitched sounds are shorter than the wavelengths of low-pitched sounds.

To produce sound, an object must vibrate, or move to and fro. Each complete to-and-fro movement—of a guitar string or tuning fork, for example—is known as one cycle. The string or tuning fork vibrates at the rate of hundreds of cycles each second, the exact rate depending on the musical note of the fork. The number of to-and-fro cycles in one second is known as the frequency. Frequencies of sounds are

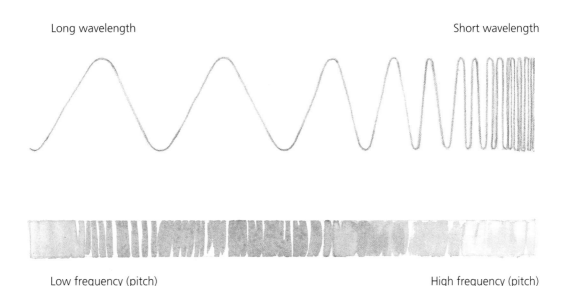

Long wavelength — Short wavelength

Low frequency (pitch) — High frequency (pitch)

TUNING FORK EXERCISE

A tuning fork not only demonstrates the nature of the oscillations that make sound. It also helps to introduce the vocabulary of sound and music—terms such as frequency and wavelength—used by acoustic engineers, musicians, vocalists, and sound therapists alike. (If you do not have a tuning fork, use any long and springy object, such as a metal ruler.) Hold the fork by its stem, so that the prongs are free to vibrate. Activate by squeezing the prongs together, then releasing them quickly. Or strike one prong on a firmly upholstered surface. Do not hit a prong on a hard edge; the tuning fork is a precise instrument that is easily damaged.

What do you see? The prongs oscillate, or vibrate to and fro. This happens so fast that your eye cannot follow them and they look blurred. What do you hear? The pure tone of a musical note, from the fork's vibrating prongs.

a major factor in determining their use in sound therapy. They are measured in units called Hertz, usually abbreviated to Hz. One Hz is one vibration or cycle per second. Tap your finger on a surface once each second and, in effect, you are making a sound with a frequency of one Hz. At such a low frequency, however, your ears detect the individual cycles as separate throbbing sounds. Only when frequencies rise above about 20 Hz do your ears perceive them as merging into one continuous sound (see page 27).

We talk of "low-pitched" sounds such as the rumble of thunder, and "high-pitched" sounds like a mouse's squeak. Low-pitched sounds have low frequencies, and high-pitched sounds have high frequencies. To give an approximate idea of frequency ranges, a rumble of thunder is 20-40 Hz (cycles per second), and a squeaking mouse about 3,000 Hz. The note called middle C, in the middle of a piano keyboard, is 256 Hz. Perhaps not by coincidence, this frequency is approximately in the centre of the frequency of human conversation, which is generally 200-400 Hz.

Large objects such as this massive temple bell in Kyoto, Japan, tend to vibrate at lower frequencies than small objects. The bell produces an immensely deep, booming ring when struck.

Sound waves and wavelengths

As the prongs of the tuning fork move to and fro, they alternately squash and stretch the air around them. Air consists of floating gas molecules. Each vibration of a prong first compresses the nearby air molecules closer together, then expands or pulls them farther apart. These "waves" of compression and expansion travel outward through the air, like ripples across a pond but in three dimensions. They are sound waves. In reality, sound waves in air consist of air molecules moving from side to side, or longitudinally. However, it is conventional to express them graphically as the smooth up-and-down motion of a typical sine wave shape, as shown on page 16.

Using the wavy-line representation, the wavelength of a sound wave is the distance between the same points in two successive sound waves, such as from one peak to the next. The wavelength of the note called middle C on the piano is 1.22 metres (48.03 inches). There is a direct mathematical relationship between wavelength and frequency. The higher the frequency, the shorter the wavelength.

The vibrations of sound pass not only through the air. They also transmit from a vibrating solid object to another object that is in contact with it. Activate the prongs of the tuning fork, and then place the stem on an object which will pick up the vibrations well, such as a hollow item of thin metal, a glass bowl, or a tabletop. Notice how sound now comes from the second object, too. You can even detect the transmission of vibrations by placing the stem of a vibrating fork on the crown of your head! In effect, sound can travel in a wave-like fashion through any medium—air, metal, glass, wood, water, and so on.

Loudness and decibels

The amount of movement in vibrating atoms and molecules determines the loudness, or volume, of a sound. In simple terms, if an air molecule vibrates to and fro only slightly, it represents a soft sound. If it vibrates more vigorously, travel-ling farther in each oscillation, it makes a loud sound.

THE SPEED OF SOUND

Sound waves travel out from their source at a speed of about 340 metres per second (760 mph). This is the speed in air, at sea level, and at a temperature of 20°C. Other substances conduct sound faster. In steel its speed is 5,000 metres per second (11,200 mph), and in glass, 5,600 metres per second (12,500 mph). Although its speed is faster, the sound usually fades away faster in these denser substances.

The speed of sound in water is 1,500 metres per second (3,350 mph). The human body is two-thirds water. The speed at which sounds pass through its tissues and organs depends largely on their water content, and this has important implications for sound's therapeutic effects.

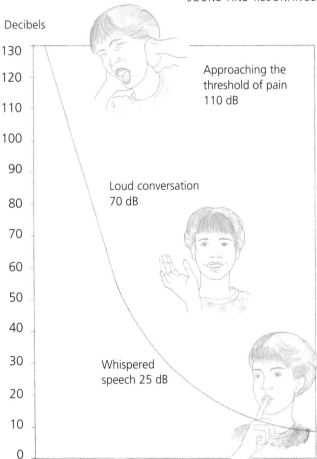

Decibels

130
120
110
100
90
80
70
60
50
40
30
20
10
0

Approaching the threshold of pain 110 dB

Loud conversation 70 dB

Whispered speech 25 dB

The decibel scale is not regular. The increase in sound intensity between 20 and 30 dB is less than the increase between 30 and 40 dB, which is less, in turn, than between 40 and 50 dB, and so on. At the upper end, a rise of a few decibels represents an enormous increase in sound intensity.

A sound's volume is another factor that has important bearings on its value in sound therapy (see page 85). Volume can be thought of as the height or amplitude of the sound wave, expressed graphically on the wave graph. It is measured in units called decibels, or dB, as shown in the chart above. Most people cannot detect sounds much below 20 dB. Conversational speech is about 60 dB, a loud orchestra or rock concert around 80-90 dB, and the threshold of pain from sound 120 dB. Living things may die if exposed to sounds above 150 dB—an ultimate expression of the power of sound and vibrations.

Sound and resonance

Each object has its own natural frequency of vibration. Tap a fine wineglass with your finger. It emits a ringing tone, its natural frequency, which is determined by its size, shape, and the material from which it is made. A trained singer could mimic the natural note of the glass and make it vibrate

SOUND WAVES AND LIGHT WAVES

In physics, sound waves are a phenomenon distinct from light waves. Sound exists as the motion of atoms and molecules and objects. It relies on matter for its transmission. Sound waves cannot pass through the nothingness of a vacuum or space.

Light waves, radio waves, X-ray waves and similar types of waves do not rely on matter. They exist as ripples or waves of electromagnetic force, rather like the invisible lines of magnetic force around a magnet. All of these waves can pass through the vacuum of space. Nevertheless, sound and light are both forms of energy, and their wave-like natures show many parallels.

This musician from Shanghai, China, plucks the strings of the lute. Some of the sound waves produced by the strings are absorbed, transformed, and re-transmitted by the lute's resonating wooden body. The result is a delicate and pleasing combination of sound waves.

in sympathy, a phenomenon known as resonance. If the singer produced sound waves of sufficient power and accuracy, the wineglass would vibrate more and more until the vibrational energy was too much for its structure—and it would crack or shatter.

In resonance, a sound source such as a plucked string produces sound waves that impart their energy to objects around. If these objects have the same natural frequency of vibration, they will be set in vibratory motion, too. Resonance is a fundamental physical principle that has many valuable applications in sound therapy (see pages 90-91).

Harmonics

We have an instinctive grasp of a sound's quality. We hear and judge sounds that are good and bad, pleasant and unpleasant, chaotic and ordered, noisy and musical. The therapeutic effects of musical sounds contrast with the negative connotations of noisy sounds. "Noise" is the result of unorderly, unorganized sound waves, whose frequencies and volumes bear no relationship to each other.

RESONANCE EXERCISE

Place two well-tuned acoustic guitars, violins, or other stringed instruments face to face, a few inches apart. Pluck a string on one, allow it to vibrate for a second or two, and damp it with your fingers. The equivalent string on the other guitar will be vibrating and emitting a faint sound, even though untouched by hand. The second string is moving as a result of the sound waves emitted by the first. This is because the two strings, being tuned together, have the same natural frequency of vibration. When one is plucked, it produces sound waves that impart their energy to objects around—including the guitar bodies and other strings. The string with the same natural frequency is most affected, and it begins to vibrate in sympathy. Such sympathetic vibration in an object, under the influence of a sound of the appropriate frequency, is termed acoustic resonance.

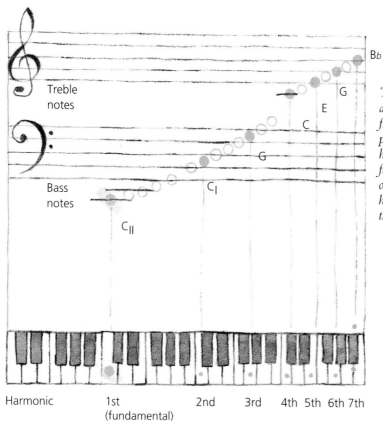

Treble notes

Bass notes

C_{II}

C_I

G

C

E

G

B♭

Harmonic

1st (fundamental)

2nd   3rd   4th 5th 6th 7th

The notes on a piano keyboard are represented by marks on a five-line musical stave. The first part of the ascending series of harmonics is shown based on the fundamental note C_{II} (the C two octaves below middle C). These harmonics are produced by a string that vibrates as shown below.

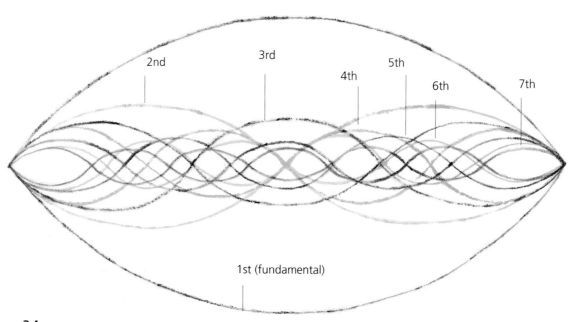

2nd   3rd   4th   5th   6th   7th

1st (fundamental)

What is special about musical sounds? They contain harmonic frequencies. A harmonic is a wave frequency that has a special relationship with another wave frequency. The relationship is usually a simple mathematical one. For example, the frequency of the harmonic may be twice the original note (which means it has half the wavelength), or four times (meaning it has one-quarter of the wavelength). There are other common ratios, as explained on page 31.

To take a visual analogy, an artist cannot create a landscape image rich in colour and shade, from a single paint pigment. Pure hues are blended into more subtle colours, shades, and tints that are pleasing to the eye. In the same way, few natural sound sources emit a "pure" note, of only one frequency. In a truly musical sound source, such as a piano or guitar string, the sound consists of many different frequencies. There is usually a fundamental frequency—the musical "note". This is produced by the string vibrating along its entire length, bowing up and down between the two fixed ends—in effect, vibrations of half a complete wavelength. The note's position on the musical scale (A, B, C, and so on) is determined by three main factors: the string's length, tension, and thickness.

The fundamental frequency or note is overlaid with patterns of harmonics. These harmonics are "in tune" with the fundamental, and the results please our ears and minds, bringing therapeutic effects. The overall movement of the string, and the sound emanating from it, is the pattern created by the fundamental and its harmonics.

Scales and octaves

A string that vibrates in one arc along its whole length produces the fundamental note, or first harmonic. If it vibrates in two sections, with a point of stillness in the centre, it produces the second harmonic note. Vibrations in three sections create the third harmonic, and so on.

The number, combination, and balance of fundamentals and harmonics determine the quality of a sound. Indeed every sound, musical or not, contains a unique pattern of fundamentals and harmonics, upon which depend its richness, clarity, quality, and individuality of tone. Vocalists and musicians spend much time and care in the cultivation of tonal quality, or timbre. Their voices and instruments are treasured for sonorous purity, brilliance, and warmth.

Harmonics which result from doubling a frequency, then doubling that, and so on, have a special place in music. They are the basis of the law of octaves, which demonstrates music's integration with universal laws of proportion and symmetry. Doubling the frequency of a sound produces the "same note on a higher level". This is the basis of the octave. The frequency of middle C, 256 Hz, doubles to produce a similar note but an octave above, written C^I (512 Hz). This frequency doubles again for C^{II}. In the opposite direction, halving the frequency of C gives C_I, a similar-sounding note but an octave below middle C.

The familiar musical scale is based on a sequence of harmonics within an octave, as explained by a vibrating string. If the fundamental is C, then the third harmonic, where the string vibrates in three sections (one-and-a-half wavelengths) gives the note G. The fifth harmonic, from a string vibrating in five sections (two-and-a-half wavelengths) produces the note E; and so on through the scale. The difference in frequency—the "gap"—between the funda-mental and the harmonic is known as the musical interval.

Hearing sounds: the ear

The human ear is a complex structure of astonishing sensi-tivity. Not only is it the organ of hearing. It also enables you to be aware of the position and movements of your head, and the direction of gravity, so contributing to your sense of balance and motion, and your ability to make smooth, coor-dinated movements (see page 28).

Your outer ear, or ear flap, merely collects sound waves. These funnel along your outer ear canal, which is about 25 millimetres (one inch) long and gently S-shaped. The sound waves impact on your eardrum, or tympanic membrane, at the end of the outer ear canal. The eardrum is like a tightly-stretched membrane of skin, measuring only 10 millimetres by 8 millimetres (0.4 by 0.3 inches). Vibrating air molecules transfer their kinetic energies to it, causing it to vibrate in sympathy with the frequencies (pitch) and amplitudes (volume) of the sound waves.

The sound waves, converted into vibrations in solids, pass along three tiny bones, known as the hammer, anvil, and stirrup. These in turn convey the vibrations to your cochlea, a fluid-filled, snail-shaped organ deep in your head, just behind your eye. The delicate cochlea transforms the physical vibrations in its fluid into electrical nerve signals, and routes the signals along the auditory nerves to the brain. In your brain, the signals are sorted and analyzed, compared with a memory bank of sounds, recognized, and identified. Most of this happens subconsciously. Patterns of sound which your subconscious deems important are brought to your attention—and you hear.

Hearing in the unborn

As a baby develops in the womb, the rudimentary ears appear within a few weeks of conception. By four-and-a-half months, the ears are complete and functional. Thus for half of its time in the womb, the baby can hear well and respond to sounds, especially music. Relaxation sessions to music for mother and unborn baby, and a peaceful musical background at the time of birth, are calming and helpful.

Scientific researches indicate that hearing in the early months of life is vitally important. In the weeks after birth, as the young baby detects each sound—especially for the first time—it moves its eyes rapidly (REM, rapid eye movement) and turns its head, attempting to locate the sound source. Even at this early stage, evidence shows that sounds are stored in the brain's auditory memory bank, providing resources for physical and mental coordination and intellectual development in later life.

The ear's frequency thresholds

Sound waves cover a vast range of frequencies, from fractions of a Hz to millions of Hz. Animals such as bats, cats, dogs, and dolphins have a wide range of hearing, extending to 200,000 Hz and above. However, the average human ear responds to a limited range of frequencies. When we talk of "sound", we refer to this limited frequency range.

THE EAR AND NATURE

The links between the shapes of parts of the ear (see page 28) and other forms in nature have long been noted and employed when devising therapeutic systems. Descriptively, the outer ear resembles the form of an inverted fetus in the womb. The cochlea's form, like the nautilus shell or sacred conch, reiterates the spiral motif of galaxies, weather-systems, and the vortices created by sound waves.

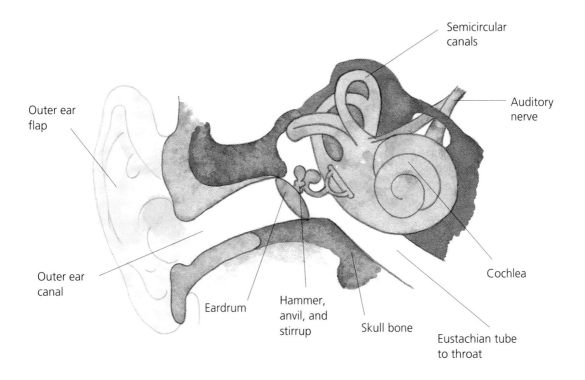

Semicircular
canals

Auditory
nerve

Outer ear
flap

Cochlea

Outer ear
canal

Eardrum

Hammer,
anvil, and
stirrup

Skull bone

Eustachian tube
to throat

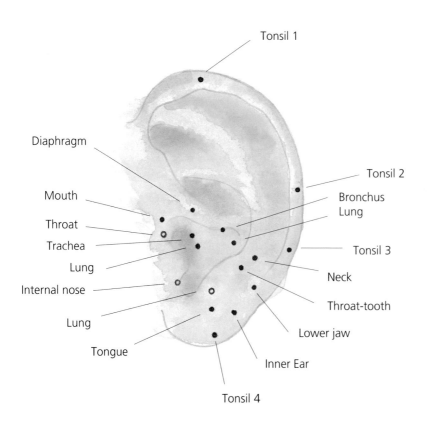

Tonsil 1

Diaphragm

Tonsil 2

Mouth

Bronchus
Lung

Throat

Trachea

Tonsil 3

Lung

Neck

Internal nose

Lung

Throat-tooth

Tongue

Lower jaw

Inner Ear

Tonsil 4

• Massage points
on outside of ear

o Points on inner
side of ear (facing
head)

Your outer ear is simply a funnel of skin and cartilage that directs sounds onto the eardrum. The cochlea turns vibrations into nerve signals and sends these to your brain. The semicircular canals help to monitor and maintain your balance.

Most people cannot detect sounds with frequencies of much less than 20 Hz, or in some cases down to 17 Hz. Below this, the vibrations can be felt by the body, but not heard. This is why you may feel the air "shake" silently during a thunderstorm. Sounds with frequencies that are too low for us to detect are known as infrasonic. Similarly, most people are unable to detect sounds with frequencies above about 20,000 Hz. In general, children can hear up to this limit; for example, they can detect the extremely high-pitched squeaks of a hunting bat's sound-radar system, which many adults cannot. The upper limit usually decreases with age, to 12,000 Hz or less by late adulthood. Sounds with frequencies which are too high for us to hear are known as ultrasonic.

The sounds you can hear are only a small extract from the immense spectrum of sound energy that is around you all the time—sounds too quiet, or low-pitched, or high-pitched, for human ears. Even though your ears cannot detect the sounds from these parts of the spectrum, other parts of your body can. Indeed, your whole body resonates to the sound energies around it, linking it to other forms of vibrational energy too. You can benefit by manipulating and fostering these links with unheard sounds in sound therapy (see page 84) .

Sound and the Universe

Auricular therapy or auriculother-apy relates every part of the body to more than two hundred points on the ear (the outer ear flap is called the auricle). Massage or acupuncture at these points can help to relieve problems in other parts of the body. A modern adaptation of this system utilizes ultrasonic sound stimulation of the ear points. Simple self-massage of the ear lobes can help to improve your auditory percep-tion, when your hearing seems uncertain or fatigued.

The Universe exists in a state of duality or two-ness, on each and every level. To and fro, expansion and contraction, centrifugal and centripetal forces, up and down, energy and matter, are all manifestations of the duality of existence. Modern astrophysics confirms this with the existence of "black holes" and "white holes" of intergalactic space, through which matter is endlessly consumed and recreated. This polarization or duality is a primal state of existence that pervades the cosmos.

Sound is no exception to the prime duality. It exists as molecular vibrations that are polarized, or in opposite motion—in other words, oscillations—of atoms, molecules, and larger objects. Sound therapy aims to create and transmit vibrational energies, which act in concert with other forms of the duality, to bring benefits and healing to the human body and mind.

The bifurcation or polarity of existence is clearly illustrated by the classic yin-yang symbol, shown on page 119. Note that the "seed" of each force lies within its opposite. Try to envisage the symbol not as a static entity, but in constant spiralling movement: the opposites perpetually merge, separate, and unite again in cycles of power and inertia.

Seeing sounds

Sound waves in air are invisible. But the work of two pioneers has brought the previously invisible world of sound before our eyes, so that we can understand it in terms of visible shapes and forms.

The eighteenth-century German physicist Ernst Chladni demonstrated the patterns that sound waves create by using a violin bow to vibrate metal plates strewn with sand grains. He showed that sound energy formed distinct patterns of grains. These were determined by the pitch of the note, although the size and thickness of the oscillating plates, and the size of the grains, also contributed to the final pattern.

In the 1960s German physician, physicist, and musician Hans Jenny investigated the science of cymatics (kymatiks), the study of wave energy. His photographic images showed the effects of sound waves passing through powders, liquids, and semi-solids, such as mercury, glycerine gel, and many other substances. The wave energy created patterns which were variously geometric, abstract, and vortical.

In many cases, as the frequency of the sound rose, the pattern became disrupted and eventually chaotic. If the frequency continued to ascend, new patterns appeared, with arrangements of symmetry and grace which characterized the new frequency band. Thus some sounds produced harmonious images, while others created visual chaos. The chief value of Chladni's and Jenny's work lies in making

SIGHT AND HEARING

The relationship between two forms of energy, sound and light, fascinates musicians, artists, and healers. Sight is your dominant sense, occupying some three-fifths of conscious attention, but your ears can detect a much wider range of frequencies than your eyes. In terms of the overall frequency bands detected, the eye responds to an approximate doubling of light wave frequencies. This doubling represents the whole of the familiar colour spectrum, from red to violet. The ear detects approximately ten times this frequency range, in the form of sound waves from very low to very high pitches.

SOUND, LIGHT, AND THE UNIVERSAL ENERGY

The human body is made of atoms which are found throughout the Universe. These atoms are of chemical elements such as carbon, hydrogen, oxygen, calcium, and iron. An element is defined partly by the vibrational rates of its atoms, and of the forces they exert on other atoms. The human organism can therefore be viewed as a manifestation of vibrational states—in a sense, a cohesion of matter, sound, and light.

visible for us, and thereby clearly demonstrating, the similarities between the patterns and forms we see in nature, and the patterns and forms inherent in sound.

Music and proportion

The mathematical ratios and relationships between musical sounds, scales, octaves, and harmonics are no isolated curiosity. They appear in many forms throughout nature, as shown by these two examples.

The interval of a fifth is particularly important. It has the next-smallest wavelength after the fundamental note; so it can be viewed as the first "child" of the "parent" in the harmonic series. The fifth is of essential importance in musical systems worldwide. As a musical manifestation of the special relationship between parent and child, it was known for thousands of years before Classical mathematicians such as Pythagoras began to express these proportions and ratios in numerical terms. Following the development of geometry in ancient times, the proportions of the principal musical intervals could at last be seen in visual form, as the regular geometric forms known as the Platonic solids (shown in the diagram on page 32).

The second example is the musical relationship termed the major sixth, in which the frequencies of the notes are in the ratio 8:5. Composers employ the major sixth because it makes the music sound positive and progressive. For example Mozart, in his opera *The Magic Flute*, introduces the principal "higher self" character Tamino with melodies based on the major sixth. This contrasts with the musical interval of a fifth reserved for Papageno, the "earthly man". The interval of the major sixth is a powerfully healing sound (see page 32).

The ratio of the major sixth has its parallel in visual terms. It is familiar to artists and architects alike as the golden section, also known as the golden mean or divine proportion. This can be represented by a rectangle in which the width compared to the length, is in the same proportion as the length compared to the sum of the width and length. It can be expressed algebraically in the manner a:b: :b:c, which means in effect: "The smaller is to the larger, as the larger is to the whole." Humans perceive it as a pleasing and harmonious relationship, used in many paintings, sculptures, and works of art, and in buildings and other structures as ancient as the Pyramids of Egypt.

The major sixth ratio also appears in a fascinating array of numbers known as the Fibonacci sequence, named after their discoverer, thirteenth-century Italian mathematician Leonardo Fibonacci (Leonardo Pisano). Each number in the sequence is the sum of the two preceding numbers: 1, 1, 2, 3, **5**, **8**, 13, 21, 34, 55 . . . The sequence is of great significance in apparently unrelated spheres, from geometry and genetics, to the natural growth patterns in plant forms and snail shells, and in art and architecture. It is also the delight of musicians, in the ordering of musical scales. These include the familiar 12-note chromatic scale of Western music, with its sharps and flats; the 5-note (pentatonic) scale consisting of the black keys on the piano, beloved of traditional folk melodies since ancient times; and the standard 7-note (diatonic) scale.

The proportional relationships of musical notes are evident in the geometric forms known as the Platonic solids. The interval of a fifth (ratio 2:3), important in musical systems around the world, and other musical ratios reappear in each form.

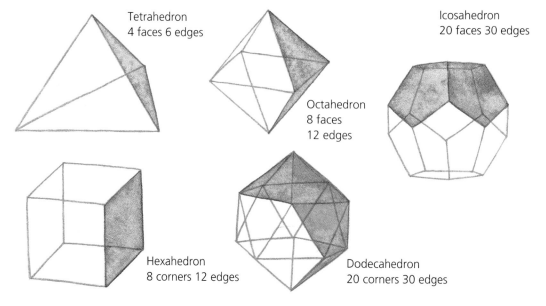

Tetrahedron
4 faces 6 edges

Icosahedron
20 faces 30 edges

Octahedron
8 faces
12 edges

Hexahedron
8 corners 12 edges

Dodecahedron
20 corners 30 edges

A courtyard of the Alhambra Palace in Granada, Spain. In this exquisite example of Moorish architecture, the proportions of the slender columns and multiple arches are founded on the classical ratios found in art, nature, and music.

Music and architecture

Music exists but fleetingly in time, and is ephemeral. Architecture is spatial, and has been described as "frozen music". Music and architecture express absolutes; they are both products of proportion in numerical expression. Great designs and constructions are musical, in the sense that both architecture and music relate to the common ratios such as the major sixth or the golden section, seen in nature and in our human-created world.

Designers of classical Renaissance times developed an unbroken tradition of study based upon arithmetic, geometry, and astronomy. They held music to be the essential ingredient. Centres of academic study, such as that of Count Bardi in Florence, pursued a monastic dedication to knowledge, artistic excellence, and moral goodness that served to nurture the flowering of human creativity. Music was the supreme discipline, providing a philosophical foundation for the visual arts grounded in a universal order.

Gaia, music, and the human form

Proportions such as the golden section thus represent relationships seen in geometry and mathematics, art and architecture, sound and music—and the human body. Taking the whole body as a fundamental, there are numerous proportions to be discovered, as shown in the illustrations opposite. Within the head, the chin-to-eyebrow distance represents a fifth interval. The tapering of human limbs illustrates the law of rhythmic diminution, clearly shown by the proportions of the hand, and the closing of the fist in a natural spiral—a living embodiment of the Fibonacci sequence.

Thus sound and music express cosmic laws. They are gateways leading from the world of our senses to the intelligible world. The laws that govern them have been embodied in the natural world since life began. Plant and animal cells are packed into space in the orders of Platonic solids; bees fashion perfectly hexagonal cylinders; conches, nautiluses, and other molluscs reveal the same harmonic proportions in the spiralling patterns of their shells; even microscopic unicellular creatures display jewel-like examples of geometric symmetry.

The human body is a living manifestation of these ratios and proportions. It is a "sounding board" awaiting the positive influences of therapeutic sounds, in which pitch and volume, resonance and harmony, play vital roles. We are an integral part of the unique and consistent geometry of our planet, demonstrated by life forms and consciousness. We are part of, and respond to, the music of Gaia.

"Listen to music.
In your creative imagination
transmute the sounds,
Into form and colour,
Dancing and alive,
A kaleidoscopic vision of energy
and beauty.
Look at a tree.
In your creative imagination,
Transmute the images,
Into rhythms and melodies,
Free and singing.
A living harmony of energy and
joy."

Listening reflection

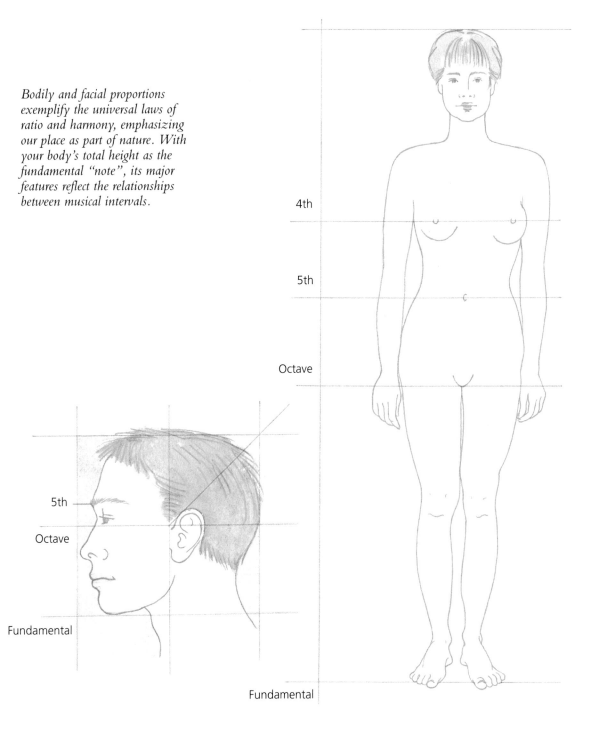

Bodily and facial proportions exemplify the universal laws of ratio and harmony, emphasizing our place as part of nature. With your body's total height as the fundamental "note", its major features reflect the relationships between musical intervals.

4th

5th

Octave

5th

Octave

Fundamental

Fundamental

TWO **THE VOICE**

Your body makes all manner of sounds, from clapping hands to stamping feet, grinding teeth, and digesting foods. But these noises are only of minor importance compared to your vocalizations—the noises you make with your vocal cords, in your voice-box or larynx. This is because the voice reflects the mental, emotional, and physical condition of a person: it is truly a parable of the soul. In the same way that the soul links the personality of the individual to the spiritual unity of the whole, the voice links the smallest wave or particle of energy to the energy of the Universe.

This chapter explains how the voice works and is controlled. It shows that discovering and releasing your voice is good for your physical health, your mental and emotional states, your appearance, your social confidence, and your communicative skills. Understanding the voice is an excellent discipline of self-awareness, and it is central to the art of listening. With careful attention you can learn to sense, from the voices of others, the unspoken meanings behind their words.

The way you use your voice gives vital insight into your complete being. Your vocalizations reveal how your energies, feelings, thoughts, and intuitions collaborate to produce your unique vocal style. This vocal style reacts to external influences as well as the feelings inside you, and it evolves through time as your emotions and past experiences accumulate and mature. Thus the voice is diagnostic as well as therapeutic (see page 105). In short: improve the use of your voice, and you will start to feel better.

Voice is built on breath. The first part of this chapter explores the mechanisms of breathing and its use in voice production, and includes some basic vocal and breathing exercises. The exercises are simple ways to extend the use of your voice and your breathing techniques, and to increase your awareness of the parts of your body involved in breathing and vocalizations. Use the exercises as ends in themselves, for meditation and relaxation, and as preparation for the more involved activities in later chapters (see, for example, pages 94, 106, and 108).

The power of a well-trained voice can move an audience to the heights of ecstasy and the depths of despair. Even when singing in an unfamiliar language, the well-crafted voice's intentions and emotions are unmistakable.

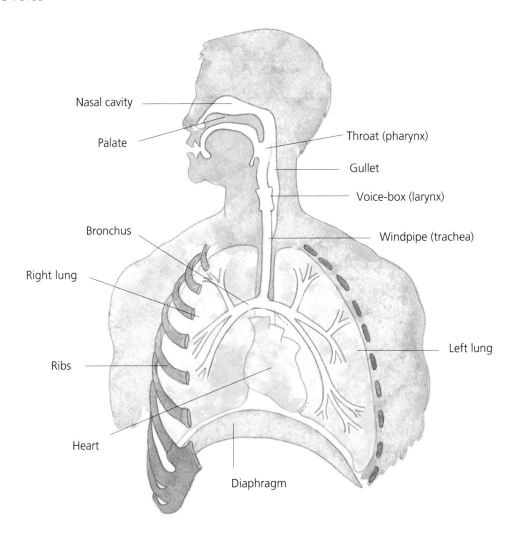

Nasal cavity

Palate

Throat (pharynx)

Gullet

Voice-box (larynx)

Bronchus

Windpipe (trachea)

Right lung

Left lung

Ribs

Heart

Diaphragm

The mechanism of breathing

Every four or five seconds, your lungs suck in fresh air containing oxygen, and exhale the poisonous wastes of carbon dioxide. This vital reflex function of respiration continues whether you are aware of it or not, whether you are in exertion, rest, or sleep. It is the body's most fundamental motivation; without it, you would suffocate and die.

Your respiratory organs include your nose and mouth, throat, windpipe (trachea), lower airways (bronchi and bronchioles), and the lungs themselves. The muscles for breathing include your chest and shoulder muscles, and in particular your diaphragm, a large muscular sheet at the base of your chest. The diaphragm marks the division between your chest and your abdomen.

Your two lungs wrap around your heart, and together these three organs fill your chest. The curved, springy ribs encircle and protect them, tilting up and down with the movements of breathing.

When you inhale, these muscles expand the lungs, drawing air into your nose and mouth, and down your windpipe. When the chest and diaphragm muscles relax, your lungs' elastic recoil makes them shrink like deflating balloons, expelling the breath in an exhalation. This means exhalation, when you speak and sing, is a passive non-muscular process that relies on the naturally shrinking lung volume.

Vocal sound production

Every musical instrument has three features that are together responsible for sound production. These are an exitor, or source of energy; a vibrator, determining sound and pitch; and resonators, adding tonal qualities. In a guitar these are the plucking finger; the string; and the guitar body, respectively. Your voice—despite any preconceptions you may hold—can be a musical instrument of great character, power, and adaptability. Its exitor is breath from your lungs; its vibrator is your vocal cords, in the voice-box or larynx; and its resonators are the air cavities and structures of your throat, mouth, nose, and sinuses.

Similarly, vocalization is divided into three main processes. These are phonation, or making the sound; resonance, or the harmonic enhancement of the sound; and articulation, the shaping and moulding and delivery of vocal sounds into the linguistic forms we call words.

As you carry out the vocal exercises in this book, always work through the physical sensations of phonation, resonance, and articulation. Feel them taking place within you. And above all, listen to yourself! Aural feedback, listening to your utterances, is a vital part of the vocalization process. Remember, it is the whole person who speaks and sings.

The vocal cords

Your vocal cords are two glistening, pearly-white protuberances on either side of the voice-box or larynx, in your neck. They are not freely vibrating, like a violin string. They are more accurately described as vocal folds because they project, shelf-like, from the larynx wall. During quiet

VOCAL ATTACK AND THE MIND'S EAR

When your breath meets your vocal cords, as sounds are initiated inside your larynx, this is sometimes described as "vocal attack". But the vocal cords are living tissue, and for all their strength and endurance, they should be caressed rather than attacked! Shouting and breathy half-singing are usually extremes to be avoided, since they tend to hold the whole body in tension. The secret, as ever, lies in your creative imagination. Just as you have a mind's eye, you also have a mind's ear. Hear sounds mentally, before you release them. This should convey the right message to your vocal mechanism, so that you say exactly what you mean.

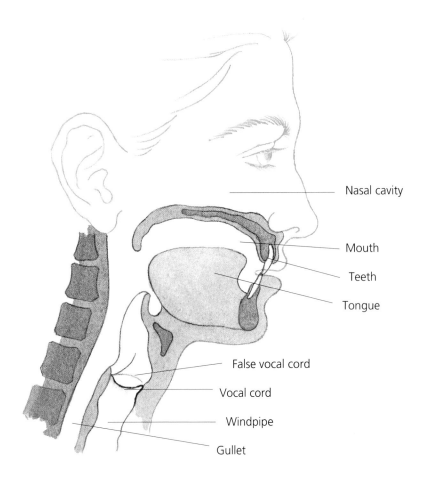

Nasal cavity

Mouth

Teeth

Tongue

False vocal cord

Vocal cord

Windpipe

Gullet

breathing, they form two long sides of a triangular-shaped orifice, the glottis, through which air reaches your lungs.

When you speak, muscles in your neck and around your larynx pull on the vocal cords so they move inward, toward the centre of the larynx, almost touching. Air must now pass through a narrow slit-shaped orifice. As it does so, it vibrates the cords. The vocal cords are companioned by a second pair of folds, sometimes described—rather unkindly—as false vocal cords, just above the true pair. Together these two pairs of folds form a womb-like vessel, the ventricle of the larynx, where sounds are initiated by the pressure of breath.

To vocalize higher-pitched notes, your larynx muscles pull on the cords and stretch them longer and tighter. Thus they vibrate at a higher frequency, in the same way that a guitar string sounds a higher note as it is tightened at the tuning

Your vocal cords lie in the voice-box or larynx, at the junction of your throat and windpipe. A complex set of muscles adjusts the shape of the larynx, to stretch or ease the tension on the cords. This controls the rate of their vibration, and alters the pitch of the voice accordingly.

peg. To increase your voice's volume, you raise the speed and pressure of air coming out of your lungs. Try speaking the same long sentence or poem in hushed tones, and then in a loud, dramatic style. See how quickly you run out of breath in the latter.

A programme for vocal exploration

In normal speech the length of your vocal cords, and the airflow past them, are adjusted by minuscule movements of the muscles in your larynx, neck, chest, and abdomen. In

A Chladni image (see page 30), from the work of Hans Jenny, of the human voice. Sand grains took up this pattern on a thin metal plate almost one-and-a-half metres (five feet) across, when the plate was vibrated by a voice singing "aaa".

fact, the whole speech system demonstrates the great variation in vocal sounds brought about by tiny alterations in your body's muscle tone and control. However, breathing and vocalizations are not simply manipulations of muscles by nerves. They involve states of awareness on many levels. This is why your voice reflects inner energies and tensions.

It is not the purpose of this book to teach you how to sing. But it should be pointed out that books explaining

RELAXATION EXERCISES

Carry out these exercises away from negative images and pressures, in comfortable clothes, temperatures, and surroundings. Try to find a quiet place, where you can hear the sounds of your own breathing and vocalizations, and where you can overcome any self-consciousness.

Lying Simply lie on your back. For comfort you may require a thin mat, and a pillow or rolled garment for your head. Feel the reassuring contact of your spine with the ground. Notice the natural rise and fall of your breath, both by watching your chest and abdomen, and by listening intently to the sounds coming from within you. Just observe and hear your body's actions. No manipulation. No control. Just breathing, and awareness of breathing.

Standing Stand upright, legs about shoulder-width apart. Become aware of the equal balance of weight carried on each side of your pelvic hip bones. Gently tilt your pelvis back and down, tucking in your "tail bone". Lift the upper part of your body from your pelvis, thus elevating your rib cage. Imagine you are holding a beach ball in each armpit, and feel the increased breathing space this provides. Your neck and head should be extended and free. Maintain this position for a minute or so. Enjoy the extension of your spine, the extra breathing space, and the feeling of poise, a happy equilibrium between calm and alertness. You are linked to earth and rising to the sun, like a well-rooted tree.

TRUST YOUR NATURAL WISDOM

When you begin the exercises described in this book, they may seem strange and awkward, and require great conscious effort. Persevere. Soon they should become easy and obvious, as your body's natural wisdom adapts to and overcomes the theoretical considerations. Eventually the exercises become as natural as breathing itself, and if you become *too* aware of them, this has a disruptive effect. The state is well illustrated by a traditional nursery jingle:
A centipede was happy quite
Until a frog in fun
Said "Pray, which leg comes after which?"
This raised her mind to such a pitch,
She lay distracted in a ditch
Considering how to run!

"methods" of singing, theories of vocal function and development, and "secrets" of technical skill, fill library shelves. The approaches in these books often give rise to conflicting assertions, which their respective supporters uphold with passion and tenacity. It follows that no one tradition encompasses the whole truth. All but the most patently ridiculous methods contain some element of value; practical wisdom can, therefore, reward discriminating study. After due investigation, one or another of the techniques may well prove to be right for you. The acid tests of "good singing" are the ease and freedom experienced by the singer in the process of vocalization, as well as the results for the listener.

These principles apply to all styles of vocalism, regardless of ethnic or cultural preferences. Therefore, as the Buddha taught, you must "work out your own salvation with diligence". Approach your vocal exploration as a path toward

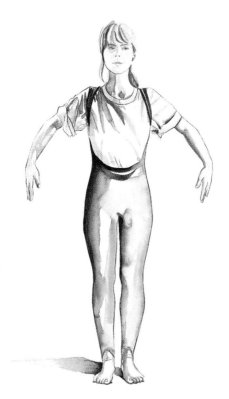

As part of the standing relaxation exercise (left), imagine that you are holding a beach ball under each arm. This encourages you to extend your shoulders and open your armpits, thereby expanding your chest volume for deeper breathing.

fulfilment and delight; and, remaining firm in your own centre, maintain your awareness and always be ready to learn from every experience.

Remember also that your whole body is your instrument. "Forced" resonance will feed back to the vibrator and impair pitch and tone. In singing, it means that unnatural forcing of the voice feeds back to the vocal cords, negating accurate control of pitch and volume. Fatigue compounds the problem. To maximize your vocal abilities and their therapeutic potential, try relaxation exercises to release the tensions accumulated by physical and emotional stress.

Basic breathing

You will encounter many ways of working with the breath: an intimidating vocabulary of technical terms, lively differences of opinion, and conflicting practices. Take heart! Bear

DYNAMIC EXERCISES

The dynamic exercises combine movement and breath control. Concentrate on the feelings of inner energy, and try to work through the different levels of awareness of your body. People often find that they cannot sustain strong, negative emotional states, such as aggression, anger, and nervousness, while they are breathing out. So at times of stress or challenge, concentrate on your exhalations.

Smiling Smile at the world! In turn, vigorously shake out your hands, arms, legs, and feet. Allow yourself a few seconds' relaxation between each shake. But keep smiling. You can do this exercise standing, sitting, or lying.

Balance Balance is important. Try the time-honoured "fashion deportment" exercise, of walking, turning, and dipping with books balanced on the head. Breathe slowly and consciously, in harmony with your body movements. This encourages smooth and graceful muscle coordination. Gracefulness is not an affectation; it is a way of loving life.

*"The powers of life in us.
Fire in our warmth and energy.
Air in our breathing and thinking.
Water in our fluids and feeling.
Earth in our substance and
stability.
These are the living forces—they
move and change, wax and
wane.
The joy of aliveness empowers us,
linking us with macrocosm and
microcosm."*

Traditional Eastern saying

in mind, whenever confusion or difficulties arise, that there are only two ways to breathe: In and Out.

What is "correct" is determined by the needs of the moment. The natural function of breathing, in itself, requires no improvement. The exercises in this book are designed to free breathing from tensions, restrictions, and counterproductive habits. Training is a matter of consciousness shading into subconsciousness. Breath control is not manipulation of nerve and muscle, but growth awareness.

Respiratory movements are involuntary, but they can be modified by conscious impulses, within certain limits. The reassuring fact is that breathing can be trusted. It continues whether you wake or sleep. Breathing relates to the biosphere of the planet. It is a process that is necessarily shared with other animal life, and it is wholly egalitarian. The

VOICE-RELEASE EXERCISE

Some people feel that they are unable to give ease and freedom to their vocalizations. They may sense that their natural voice is in some way blocked, trapped, or suppressed. Try this voice-release exercise as part of your vocal programme.

Sitting on your buttocks, fold and curl your body into a tight compact knot of arms and legs; try to condense yourself into as small a mass as possible. Trap your breathing and vocalizing organs at the centre of the mass. As a last effort, breathe out to make the space you occupy even smaller. Hold the position for a moment. Then simultaneously breathe in and stretch out, quickly and vigorously. Release some of your voice into a powerful "ugh", using the deepest sound you can find far within yourself. Maximize and enjoy the stretch. Rest for a moment. Repeat the exercise up to ten times. Each time, reach deeper within, and project your released voice more strongly and farther. Notice that you come to involve your whole body in the vocalization, particularly your pelvis and diaphragm.

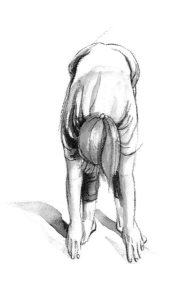

COMPLETE BREATH EXERCISE

1 Stand with your legs comfortably shoulder-width apart, facing forward, arms and hands loose by your sides. Centre yourself, checking your posture. Breathe out as far as you can. When you feel "empty" of air, cough—and prove to yourself that you have hidden reserves.
Try to touch the floor, bending your knees if necessary. Hold the out-breath for a few seconds.

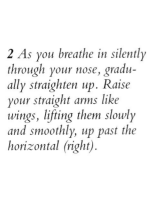

2 As you breathe in silently through your nose, gradually straighten up. Raise your straight arms like wings, lifting them slowly and smoothly, up past the horizontal (right).

3 As you complete the movement and the in-breath, bring your hands together above your head, in an attitude of prayer (above). Hold the inhalation. Be aware of the exchange of energies and the renewal of life in every cell of your body.

adaptation of the "complete breath" exercise described on these two pages is a fine vehicle for relaxation and meditation, and also wonderful preparation for singing.

Everyday vocalizations

People do not "work" music. They "play" it. When you sing with your vocal instrument, approach it with a sense of play and fun.

De-armouring Begin by vocalizing in your daily life while you walk, bend, stretch, and turn. Hum quietly, sing a favourite ditty, or simply mouth tuneful "da-de-das". Importantly, note how your voice responds when a certain part of your body is involved in the motions. For example, does it tend to become quieter, or more faltering, when you bring into action your neck muscles, or perhaps your hips? This can help you to locate areas of "armouring"—parts of your body that seem to be stiff, tense, and tough, covered with "armour". Such armour is often the residue of painful (usually forgotten) experiences, frozen into muscular resistance. Try to give voice to these frozen feelings, in order to dissolve them and free yourself (see page 73).

Dance Dancing of any style is strongly recommended. Expertise is not necessary. What is important is that you move rhythmically and adopt a singing pattern which is naturally deep, free, and relaxed. If you are shy and inhibited, try dance-singing with a partner or in a group, to open the "cage" of self-consciousness and inhibition.

Singing with others With family members or friends, agree to a singing session when all communication will be sung—no matter how! A coffee break or mealtime is ideal. Try styles such as opera, or blues, or old-time vaudeville. You may well be surprised at the vocal resources revealed by yourself and your companions; and the laughter generated is itself therapeutic, and a wonderful social lubricant.

Voice resonance Sound waves resonate the walls or boundaries of a space. In a limited volume, they and their reflections also interact with each other to produce "pulses" of

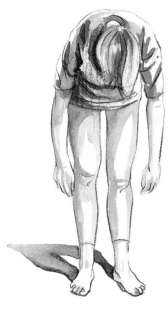

4 *When you are ready, silently breathe out through your mouth, and lower your straight arms slowly until they are just below horizontal. Quickly release your remaining breath as an audible sigh, and allow your upper body to flop down so that you bend forward at the hips, head hanging (above). Consciously release all the "used-up" air you no longer need. Relax for a moment and repeat the whole exercise.*

sound, called reverberations. You can experience this by singing with your head near the corner of a wall, or singing in the bath, or by cupping your hands over your ears while you listen to your own voice.

Vowels and consonants

Vowel sounds are the tonal qualities of the voice carried by an uninterrupted flow of breath. Consonants result from interrupting the flow of breath. The continuing sounds of vowels are determined by the shape of the resonating spaces within the throat and mouth, and further enriched by harmonic "overtones" produced in the sinuses. There are many subtle variations lying between the five principal vowel letters in English, a–e–i–o–u. In fact, in standard English there are well over one hundred vowel variations!

"The usefulness of a container lies within the shape of its emptiness."

Hindu proverb

For the second part of the physical breathing exercise described on page 49, hold your clasped hands slightly away from the small of your back (left). Then bend at the waist as far forward as you can, while raising your hands above your head (right).

PHYSICAL BREATHING EXERCISE

This two-part routine coordinates breathing movements with minor "physical jerks" of your other body parts. It is a useful preparation for more vigorous physical exertions, and it encourages the development of smooth respiration.

Stand comfortably with your arms loose by your sides, feet shoulder-width apart. Clasp your hands behind your neck. Check that your head, neck and spine are in full vertical alignment, and breath out. Keeping this posture, bend sideways at your waist to your right, so that your right elbow points to the ground. Feel the stretch in your left side. Breathe in and hold. Then breathe out as you straighten to the upright. Rest for a moment, and repeat the movement, to the left side. Try about ten or twenty complete left-right movements, paying attention to how your breathing slots into your whole body movements.

Rest for a minute or so, then move on to part two of the exercise. Commencing as before, clasp your hands behind your back, not touching your back but about 20 centimetres (8 inches) from the small of your back. Breathe in and hold the air. Keep hands linked and arms straight, bend forward at the waist to bring your clasped hands as far over your head as possible. Breath out and rest momentarily in this position. Then straighten again, inhaling and feeling your lungs filling with freshness. Repeat the bending movement ten to twenty times. Finally, lie quietly for a minute or two, paying attention to how your breathing recovers.

As the converse of vowels, consonants result from stopped breath that is suddenly released. Your most flexible muscle, your tongue, is the prime releaser and shaper of consonant sounds. Repeat the series of consonants "lee, tee, nee, kee, gee" and feel how your tongue releases the sound from farther and farther back into your mouth and throat. Discover the resonances and harmonics of vowel sounds for

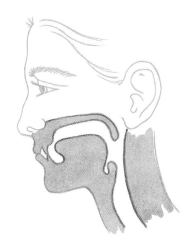

HUMMING EXERCISE

Explore reverberations within your body's own air chambers by humming, the vocal exercise par excellence! We naturally hum when contented, and happy, and absorbed, and at one with the situation. There are three equally important humming positions. Try each one in turn. Why not right now? The first position is with your lips closed, the simple "mmmmmm". You can merge it into open vowel sounds, such as "mmmaaah, mmmeeeh, mmmooo". The second is with the tip of your tongue against the ridge (alveolar ridge) toward the front of the roof of your mouth, producing the "nnnnnn". Again, open and merge it into vowel sounds like "nnnaaah, nnneeeh, nnnooo". Third is with the rear part of your tongue raised to the soft palate, toward the back of the roof of your mouth. It produces the more nasal "ngngngng", opened into "ngngaaah, ngngeeeh, ngngngooo".

When humming "mmm", your lips are closed and your tongue lies at rest on the floor of your mouth (above). Feel the vibrations in your palate (the roof of your mouth).

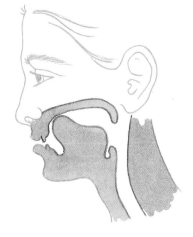

The "nnn" hum is produced when your tongue touches the hard front part of your palate (above). The vibrations may spread up into your ears.

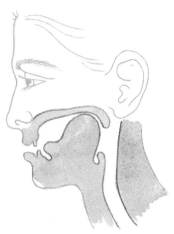

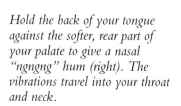

Hold the back of your tongue against the softer, rear part of your palate to give a nasal "ngngng" hum (right). The vibrations travel into your throat and neck.

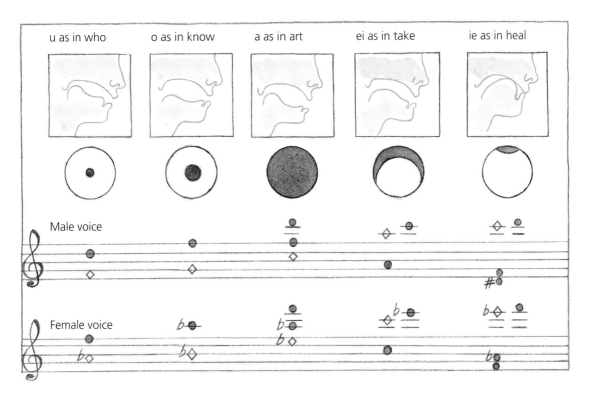

u as in who   o as in know   a as in art   ei as in take   ie as in heal

Male voice

Female voice

Five so-called Italian vowels form the basis of good vocal practice. The top illustrations show the positions of mouth and tongue. Beneath are diagrammatic representations of the "feel" of the vowel shape, combining lip and tongue positions as seen from the front. Under these are the pitches of the whispered vowels on the musical scale, for average male and female voices respectively.

yourself, by whispering the vowel series a-e-i-o-u. Cover a musical-like "scale" of sounds which has a range of about one-and-a-half octaves. Practise singing these quietly, then louder. To ensure verbal clarity, there is no better exercise than rhythmically voicing your way through a series of consonantal formations, but in a manner which is whispered, slowed down, and exaggerated. This brings many of your facial and throat muscles into action, with rejuvenating effects. Lively articulation is good for your looks, too!

CONSONANT EXERCISES

To ease tension or tiredness in your tongue, stretch it outward while yawning. (Notice the grace with which cats perform this exercise!) The inner feelings of a yawn are the sensations experienced in good singing. Sometimes your tongue may feel "lazy". To cure this, sing or say vowel sounds preceded by the consonant L, such as "looh", "low", "laah", "lay". Now do the same, with the back of your hand about seven centimetres (two-and-a-half inches) in front of your mouth—and on the initial "L" of each syllable, touch the back of your hand with your tongue.

"The soul is in the tongue; the tongue is a rudder or steering-oar with which a man steers his course through the world."

Ancient Egyptian belief

The music of the world comprises a whole family of related languages, each with a vocabulary, a grammar, and a literature. Many of these languages have a written script of great beauty. In all civilizations music has been considered so treasured and meaningful, that music books and musical instruments have been lavishly decorated with rare pigments, precious metals, and gemstones, by generations of skilled and dedicated craftspeople.

Today, we are most familiar with the visual representation of western European music as depicted in this book, with its five-line staves, and notes such as minims and quavers. The printed symbols of music have a history spanning centuries of gradual development, spurred by changes made necessary by musical innovation and evolution of musical instruments.

Beyond the individual, music has remarkable power to unite and motivate groups and communities. Whole nations are united and enthused by music at the spectacles of state ceremonies. Marching bands, massed choirs, rock concerts, pop marathons, and full-throated sports supporters in paroxysms of victory or defeat—these are all examples of music arousing and concentrating private emotions into a single energy, intense enough to elevate the shared experience to a level of ecstasy.

Music and nature

A world without natural and familiar sounds would be alien indeed. Can you imagine weathers without the music of the wind, or the rhythm of pattering rain? An environment without the wave sounds of the sea, the murmur of a river, or the gush of a waterfall? No buzzing bees or cheeping crickets? We may term these intrinsically beautiful sounds the "music of Gaia", after the Greek goddess of the Earth, Gaia, who has become associated with modern movements toward nature, conservation, and enlightenment.

No Gaia music is more generally known and loved than bird song. It has many parallels with our own music. Bird song is complex, prolonged, and rhythmic; it often celebrates courtship and territory, like our own songs of home

"Orpheus with his lute made trees,
And the mountain tops that freeze,
Bow themselves when he did sing.
To his music plants and flowers ever sprung,
As sun and showers there has made a lasting spring."

William Shakespeare

The Tree of Jesse, a medieval work reflecting the importance of music in life. The musicians, playing a range of instruments, sit between the learned men and the mother with her infant above, and the crowned king below.

and care; birds seem to sing simply for the joy of singing; each bird species has recognizable characteristics, modified in some cases by local differences of musical "dialect"; and each bird develops unique variations on its inherited song pattern, rather like the tradition of folk songs transmitted among human communities.

The beneficial effects of music in nature are legend, especially in the ancient East. Folk traditions relate intriguing stories of music promoting fertility and rich harvests. The Indian city of Vrindavan is renowned for its gracious green beauty, attributed to the life-giving flute music of Krishna. Mian Tan Sen, sixteenth-century court musician to the Emperor Akbar of Lahore, could not only cause trees to grow and blossom; he supposedly changed the weather to benefit the imperial plantations by intoning the appropriate chants. In southern India, the natural music of humming and buzzing insects is believed to ensure the healthy sprouting of the sugar cane.

Modern science lends its support. Plants grow faster when music is "piped" over fields or into greenhouses. Carefully conducted experiments prove that germination, growth, flowering, fruiting, and seed yield are affected by sound

A musical phrase from a common garden songster, the blackbird. Each bird has its own "song-print", a unique vocal style and phrasing, which enables human experts to identify not only the species, but the individual bird.

waves, particularly musical sounds in the low frequency range, from 100 Hz to 600 Hz. Farm animals and pets show response to music; cows give more milk when music is relayed to the milking parlour; some racehorses fret if the transistor radio is removed from their stables.

If plants and animals respond, why not humans? Under the gloss of modern civilization, often thin and flaking, we are the evolutionary products of nature. There is no reason why we should be apart or immune. We have a growing realization that planetary life is a web of interaction, each part depending on another. We can train ourselves to recover an ancient understanding in which music symbolizes and expresses the principle of mutual communication. Music, understood spiritually, is reverence for life.

Nature sound therapy

Over many years, therapists and psychologists have helped their patients to observe how the music of nature affects the emotions and the spirit. You may be able to discover and adapt these observations for your own circumstances. For example, try the musical tinkling of running water—a small brook, fountain, or waterfall—if you have overactive, disturbed, or pent-up emotions, such as jealousy, frustration, and anger. Picture the water washing and cleansing, to leave your mind shining bright and uncluttered, like the scoured

NATURE-MUSIC EXERCISE

We need no evidence for the soothing and spirit-raising benefits of natural music, such as our shared joy in bird song. As a useful awareness procedure, go out into the open air and focus your ears and mind on the natural sounds that surround you. Make a list of those you hear, and your reactions to them. Appreciate singing birds, humming insects, rustling leaves, swishing grass, barking dogs, and whinnying horses. Which are most obvious, and which are hidden away? Do you tend to notice sounds by volume, loudest first, or by frequency, low-pitched first?

pebbles of a stream bed. Likewise, the whisper of a gentle breeze can blow away mental dust and cobwebs.

Some people find that if they have been under pressure and stress, the sound of the wind (especially strong wind) is frustrating, even tormenting. If this happens to you, it may help to go out into the wind and face it head-on, rather than sheltering indoors, where its disembodied mufflings can gnaw away at your subconscious.

As technology uncovers more about the secrets of why such sounds have a strong impact on our being, bird song may well become a recognized holistic therapy. Certainly there can be no better prescription for stress than a session of, for instance, 15 minutes of blackbird, thrush, and robin song, in equal parts!

NATURE-LISTENING EXERCISE

Follow the nature and spirit of this text, as an introduction to the wonders of Gaia music, and the sharing of its joys and sorrows with other living beings.

"Listen! First, seek the silence. If you can find a meditation place, under the trees, by the river, on the mountainside, or in a tranquil garden—Good! If not, enter your inner land-scape, the garden planted and cherished by your creative imagination."

"Listen! Let the sky, the light, the earth, the water, the rocks, the plants and animals, SING from their hearts into yours. You will not need to 'make' yourself sing, or know 'how'. If you have an open heart and love in your listening, the song will happen, like the opening of a flower."

"Listen! Perhaps it is for you alone. Perhaps you can share it with another listener, or with many, or with the soul of a dying friend. You may remember it forever. Or for a day, or for an hour. That does not matter. Its source has no end. It is enough that you have listened. You can return to the song-world whenever your heart answers its call. Only listen!"

Basics of musical form

Musical form as we know it today in the West was brought to full development in the eighteenth century. But it must be stressed that music of whatever style has formal elements in its design. An awareness of these "shapes in sound" can aid your appreciation of music and its therapeutic effects, as you learn to recognize the different forms and understand their inner meanings.

One note from a simple drum, or from the lone string of a piano, violin, or guitar, may be a musical sound. But the constructional unit of music, as in speech, is the phrase. Originally a phrase was a group of notes or words (a "line") which could be sung in one breath, without discomfort. Myriad examples of the phrase are found among traditional hymn tunes and folk songs.

Two successive phrases take the form of "question-and-answer" symmetry and are described as a musical sentence; this is the essential motif of the melody or "tune". Our natural pleasure in repetition and contrast build musical sentences into the four-line verse structure familiar from countless popular songs, from opera to blues, from Cole Porter to the Beatles. This two-fold symmetry expresses a complementary duality. Its inner meanings of equilibrium, containment, and completion can have therapeutic effects on loss of mental or emotional balance, shock, fear of isolation or solitude, and restlessness and lack of concentration.

In contrast, a musical form with the ternary structure has two similar musical statements with a differing middle section. This is found in many popular songs as the "middle eight" or "instrumental break". With its inner promise of a new beginning, and of transformation without destruction, this form can have beneficial effects on problems caused by fixed ideas, inertia, lack of adaptability, and fears of new events or open spaces.

A third example is the rondo form, based on the ballad or story-song with verses linked by a recurring chorus. The inner meanings here are of excursions and homecomings, relating the old and the new, and resolving the strange and the familiar. Musical passages with the rondo form may benefit pessimism, loss of faith or courage, bitterness, cynicism, and resentment.

A fourth example is often called the air and variations. It is a central musical statement, expressed several times in as many ways and "decorations" as the composer or player can devise. The inner meaning reflects the multiple self—the different facets of the personality that appear in different

MUSICAL FORM EXERCISE

Sing through one of your favourite songs a few times. It can be a hymn or folk tune, stage song or popular composition; ideally it should be fairly slow and lyrical. If you cannot choose one, begin with the well-loved traditional song *Swing Low, Sweet Chariot*.

First, read and study the musical form. Each line is a phrase, and the first pair of phrases makes a musical sentence that establishes the melody. The second sentence virtually repeats, and reaffirms, the melody. Lines five and six depart with a questioning approach. The final lines both answer the question and bring the tune satisfyingly full circle.

Next, analyze the words, their meanings and pronunciations, and the story they tell. In your mind's ear, note how the musical notes complement the lyrics, with their twists and emotional content.

Then sing through the song a few times. Notice how the structures within the words and the melody are reflections of the emotional pattern from which the song springs. Can you imagine singing the same melody, but with a statement rather than a question in lines five and six? Or with the last two lines missing? Try this process with some of your favourite songs, especially traditional words and melodies that have pleased the generations, and withstood the stringent tests of time.

SWING LOW, SWEET CHARIOT

Swing low, sweet chariot,
Coming for to carry me home.
Swing low, sweet chariot,
Coming for to carry me home.
I looked over Jordan and what did I see,
Coming for to carry me home?
A band of angels coming after me,
Coming for to carry me home.

SUNG POETRY EXERCISE

This exercise and its many derivations encourage you to reintegrate poetry and music, and to combine them with physical motion. It helps to speed your reactions, remove stress from your vocal mechanisms, and dissolve any inhibitions you may have, associated with singing. It is an excellent exercise for vocal confidence and coordination of body, mind, and voice.

Select one of your favourite, much-loved poems. You will need a large inflated balloon, and plenty of uncluttered space in which to move, while your attention is focused elsewhere. Tap the balloon into the air, and keep it airborne with light touches from your fingers, head, knees, and toes. At each contact, sing a word from the poem, concentrating on perfect synchronization of sound and touch. You should quickly realize just how little physical effort is required, but paradoxically, how much is demanded of your vitality in body and mind. Both the balloon and your vocalizations respond best to delicacy and precision of impact. As your skill develops, you can devise other ways of using this exercise. You might try singing a musical scale while keeping the balloon aloft, or bouncing the balloon against a wall while singing, or working with a partner or in a group.

situations and relationships. Experiencing music of this form, for example, in jazz, can help conditions involving shame and guilt, fear of self-expression or punishment, self-imposed limitations, and self-hatred.

Poetry and music

Poetry and music have one fountain-head of expression: your voice. Through poetry, as through song, you are able to express feelings that elude definition in everyday speech and vocabulary. You find acceptable outlets for negative attitudes and emotions that would otherwise paralyze or swamp

"All sorrows can be borne if you put them into a story."

Isak Dinesen

your psyche. This notion finds extreme expression in the various types of primal and scream therapies (see Useful addresses, page 122).

In many societies, this dual speech-song function of the voice is falsely separated into analytical and emotional: "head and heart", "matter and spirit", "fact and fancy". However, think of your voice as a two-way mirror, bringing music and words into a single focus; and be equally at home in each modality. Sing the praises of poems! Express melodies in celebratory verse!

Poems can be profound, provoking, or just fun! They can be painstakingly constructed or extemporized; they can be read, spoken aloud, or combined with music, dance, and visual art. Poetry can be intensely personal and private, or for sharing; for good times or bad; and above all, for recognition, blessing, and delight.

The arts of silence and laughter

Sound therapies have special places for two modes of expression that come from deep within your subconscious: silence, and laughter.

Silence is not a gap to be filled at all costs, but a living presence to be cultivated, a comfort, and a therapy. Singers learn to treasure silence and are trained to avoid unnecessary chatter before a performance. And think of the communicative power of mime! Some of the world's greatest mime artists combine the arts of silence and laughter, as they clown to the world's amusement. Observe how much mime is used quite naturally, in animated conversation, in teaching and public debate, in everyday situations, in the store or cafe, on the street or transportation. Usually people's gestures reinforce their words, but occasionally their body language contradicts their most vehement spoken communications. Which, do you think, comes nearer to the truth?

It is difficult to over-emphasize the importance of laughter, for body and soul. Laughter turns the world upside down, inside out, and back to front. It nourishes sanity and

"The birth of language was the birth of humanity. Each word was the sound-equivalent of an experience connected with an internal or external stimulus, a focus of energies, in which took place the transformation of reality into the vibrations of the human voice— the vital expression of the soul. Through these vocal creations, humanity took possession of the world."

Lama Gorinda

Ceremonial horns ring out at a Welsh eisteddfod. These festivals have ancient roots and bring together musicians, dramatists, dancers, and actors, who merge the language of music with other performing arts.

SILENCE EXERCISES

Have you ever immersed yourself in real silence? In this noise-polluted world of planes, trucks, radios, and heavy machinery, it is becoming more difficult. Yet with ingenuity and planning, it is still possible. Why not experiment by allowing yourself a small measure of silence each day? As little as five or ten minutes will prove a challenge, but it should also prove refreshing and relaxing. Approach it not as a refusal to communicate, but as a period of heightened listening. Episodes of silence help to reinvigorate and refine your voice, your vocabulary, and your speech patterns.

Capitalize on the communicative power of mime. If you are preparing a public statement, the verbal presentation of an idea, or the lines of a play or poem, try miming the meaning of the script. Impart your message silently, by gesture and body language.

explodes every kind of pomposity. Laughter from the heart, no less than tears, can dissolve the shells of loneliness and insecurity. It is immensely therapeutic. And it is a scientifically proven, harmless pain-killer, since it releases the body's natural pain-killing substances, known as endorphins, from the brain. Whenever reality is threatened by false solemnity, or commonsense is invaded by the prattle of so-called expertise and officialdom—bring in the clowns! Cultivate the approach of smiling from within. Look for the best, or at the least, see the funny side. Be light-hearted, radiant, and sparkling; glow with health; put difficulties into perspective; glide toward enlightenment. All therapies call for a "light touch", and laughter is exactly that: the touch of light.

Music and the spiritual quest

A time-honoured feature of many cultures around the world, widespread in space and time, is the tradition of shamanism. The shaman, man or woman, is believed to communicate directly with the spirit world, often while in a

USING CHANTS

Begin to explore the use of chants with those shown here and on the next page, and progress to creating your own. Follow your mind as the repetitive sound of the chant focuses it inward to your soul and spirit.

A MOUNTAIN CHANT

Seated at home behold me,
Seated amid the rainbow,
Seated at home.
Lo, here in this holy place.
Yes, seated at home, behold me!
In life unending and beyond it,
Yes, seated at home, behold me!
In joy unchanging,
Yes, seated at home, behold me!

A SHARING CHANT

I add my breath to your breath,
That our days may be long on the Earth,
That the days of our people may be long,
That we may be one person.
That we may finish our roads together,
May my Father bless you with life
May our life-paths be fulfiled.

trance-like or ecstatic state. Shamanism is often concerned with healing and divining, as well as with other community concerns, such as rain for crops. Sounds—of the shaman's own vocalizations, of the voices of participants and onlookers, and of drums and other instruments—are paramount. They are often in the form of repetitive chants.

The shamanistic healer is therefore the link between the people and the spirit world. Through time, these individuals have been called to priestly roles, for whom times of crisis and tests of courage are the initiatory rites of passage to the privilege of mystical healing powers. When song rises from the heart, the healer and the people are of one spiritual body. The spontaneous release of the sacred chant bestows upon the healer and the community a power that is reinforced by every subsequent repetition. From the memories of trial and anguish, the healer can "sing into life" others who face sickness and death. Such chants and songs are almost living beings, "comrades in loneliness", sung by the breath of men and women for whom speech no longer suffices. One healer explained: "How many songs I have within me, I cannot tell you . . . there are so many occasions of joy and sorrow when the desire comes upon me to sing . . . all my being is song."

Deep in the innermost mind of the shamanistic healer is the doorway or passage which leads to the spirit world. It is through this door—closed most of the time, to the uninitiated—that the singer is admitted to the mysteries of song and healing. Healing songs are born in stillness and silence, while the song-maker meditates upon "beautiful things" in the surroundings, such as the forest or the mountain. The melodies, rhythms, and words rise like bubbles from the depths of the ocean, seeking air in order to release their power. Such songs from the unconscious realms are not easily won; a healer must enter the unknown heights and depths of joy, pain, loneliness, and fear. This is an heroic adventure, yet it is said that "only to one who is humble does the dream come, and contained within the dream there is always a song".

Each of us has the capacity to develop at least an echo of these healing powers. The dream which contains your song may be for you alone, revealing a unique and personal chant, your own "life signature". Or the dream may manifest as a healing song for a sick neighbour, a gathering call for the local group, an anthem for the whole nation, or music that shakes the world.

GROUP MUSIC-MOVEMENT EXERCISE

This group exercise for three to six people combines music, movement, listening, and general awareness. Practise it in an area which affords enough space for everyone to move about freely, and where you can be quiet and undisturbed. A shared feeling of sensitivity and trust is important. Before you begin, check that each of you has sufficient personal space. Ensure that each person can stretch out arms, unhindered in every direction, from one standing spot.

First, each member of the group sings an item of his or her choice—a popular song, hymn tune, traditional ballad, television jingle, even an improvized song—all at the same time! Keep your voice volumes within previously agreed limits. This helps each participant to maintain personal identity in the face of possible distractions, without shouting!

Second, continue to sing, and also make improvized movements, using the whole of the working area. Take care to respect each other's personal space, so that no one is impeded. Remember to keep singing and keep moving throughout this phase of the exercise. It's a good test of physical and mental adaptability as well as agility!

Third, sing and move as before—but now in slow motion, and with each person's eyes closed. Sense your relative positions by sound alone. The intense concentration that this requires will help to deepen your awareness of everyday movements and sounds, to the extent that the exercise becomes an "active meditation".

A NAVAJO NIGHT-HEALING CHANT

Happily, I recover,
Happily my interior becomes cool,
Happily I go forth.
My interior feeling cool, may I walk,
No longer in pain, may I walk,
As it used to be long ago, may I walk,
Happily with abundant clouds, may I walk,
Happily with abundant showers, may I walk,
Happily on a trail of pollen, may I walk,
Happily may I walk.

A SIOUX SUN CELEBRATION CHANT

A voice,
I will send,
Hear me,
The land,
All over.
A voice,
I am sending.
Hear me!
I will live!

ACTIVE LISTENING EXERCISE

Listening to and understanding the language of music can heal, especially when the music embodies your deepest feelings and aspirations. Listening from your heart, not with your mind, is a form of meditation. If you truly listen to great music, and allow it to touch your heart, you will be surprised at how therapeutic the experience can be. It can help you during times of mental stress, ill health, or emotional upset.

Choose a personal small library of recordings with great care. Select only those pieces which truly "speak" to your mind and heart. Choose directly, from within you, regardless of expert opinion or fashion. Settle on music that you may not comprehend, as yet; but which you suspect will provide eventual fulfilment. Avoid music that you instinctively feel may leave you empty and unmotivated.

Find a comfortable sitting position, which allows you to relax with your eyes closed, while remaining wide awake and alert. Select one of the musical pieces, of about eight or ten minutes. Play it through once, just listening. Simply allow the music to "soak" in. Visualize the sounds in shapes and colours that filter through your skin into your bloodstream, bones, and nerves.

After a pause, listen to the piece again. Use your arms and hands to express what you hear. Feelings, thoughts, and reveries evoked by the music should flow from your heart into your shoulders, representing your will, and then into your forearms, which represent your emotions. The feelings enter your hands and fingers to the tips, signifying your intellectual activity—and out into your world.

Finally, add your voice to the movements. Hum, sing, or use your voice in any other way. You may well be astonished at how easily the movements and sounds flow, and how you feel lifted and inspired afterward.

"The singer alone does not make the song.
There has to be someone who hears.
One man opens his throat to sing,
The other sings in his mind."

From *The Broken Song* by Rabindranath Tagore

Your voice links the conscious and unconscious levels of your being. You can carry out explorations, investigations, and exercises that help to bring together these two levels of existence into harmonious relationships that can be powerfully therapeutic. This chapter shows you how to use vocal and other sounds, and movements, in conjunction with your mental abilities and emotions, to look inward, and discover more about your inner self. With enhanced self-knowledge, you are set on the path to healing.

The advice and guidance in the following pages is exactly that—it is not intended to be hard-and-fast instruction. Read through the different sets of activities and exercises, and select the ones which seem most suited to your own situation. Do not be afraid to modify the exercises by following your instincts and your creative imagination.

FACIAL EXPLORATION EXERCISE

As an initial familiarization exercise, get to know your own face—by touch. With your eyes closed, explore the bone structure of your face using your fingertips, giving particular attention to your nose, brow, cheek, and jaw bones. Carefully feel the forms beneath your skin and flesh. Take your time. Become familiar with the contours and inner skeletal strength, beneath the features that you know so well by sight. With your thumbs, find the ends of your lower jaw, beneath your ear lobes. Follow the line of the jaw bone, past a sharp angle and then a curved depression, continuing this exploration until your thumbs meet under the chin. Your facial expressions and vocalizations are supported by this inner skeletal stability

Carry out the explorations as you hum, speak, sing, and articulate. Feel the movements, vibrations, and resonances that produce the sounds.

Music is the gateway to the path of personal discovery. Children, especially, have an open attitude, and are often more willing than adults to express themselves through instruments and song.

Are any areas sensitive or tender to touch? If so, work gently on them, moving your thumbs in small circles, to release tensions held there (see page 78).

Singing musical scales

You may recall singing the musical scales while at school, to the tune of the typical eight-step octave, starting on the note of middle C: *doh ray me fa so la te doh*. But try to think of scales as ladders or stairways, spiralling up and down the octaves of sound. Cultivate their enjoyment. Use them for freedom of access to further musical sounds, for all melodies go up and down these rungs on the sonic spectrum.

OWN NAME EXERCISE

A name is a stream of connected sounds, but because it represents a person, the sounds are invested with meanings, memories, and assumptions. Say your name several times, slowly and carefully. Be aware of the movements involved, your breath, and the shapes and flexibility of your tongue and lips. Next, repeat your name in its natural rhythm: for example, *Mary Elizabeth Brown*. Notice how the stresses form a rhythmic pattern: *Ma-ry-E-liz-a-beth-Bro-own*. Speak the rhythm. Clap it, walk it, finger- and toe-tap it. Now turn your name-rhythm into a musical phrase by singing it as a song. Experiment with different tunes. Does one feel "right"? Fine; but remember the "right" tune could differ tomorrow, for this exercise reveals how you feel about yourself right now! Some guidelines on interpretation:

Ma-ry E-liz-a-beth Brown You probably feel poised, balanced, alert, efficient. Little silences are signs of precision.
M'ry 'Liz-a-beth Brow' Minimal vowels, and less definite pitch and rhythm, give the impression of slight deterioration. You may feel sad, insecure, and lonely.
Ma—ry E—li—za—beth Bro—wn The expansive mood and single-breath delivery, rising with confidence, indicates vitality and optimism. Your ambitions are based on clear ideas, although you may be restless and would benefit from relaxation and meditation.

Finally, use your creative imagination to hear, inwardly, your name spoken by the wisest, kindest voice you have ever heard. It will be the sound of your healed self.

WRONG NOTES

There are no intrinsically wrong notes. There are, however, perfectly good notes in the wrong place at the wrong time, because, for equally mistaken reasons, they have been misplaced. Indeed, notes which seem most excruciatingly wrong are those nearest to being right! However, such misplaced energies are less resonant and harmonious than the tuneful sounds around them. They are quickly exhausted and reabsorbed into the sonic reservoir.

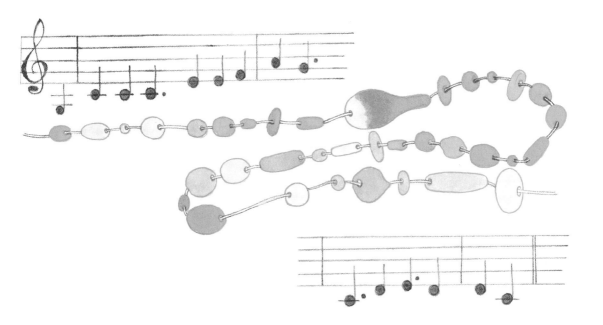

This representation visualizes the "sound necklace" for the folk sea tune Shanendoah, *with a loose musical representation of the notes. The colours of the beads represent the pitch or frequency of each note, with higher notes being lighter. The bead shapes indicate vowel sounds, opening and closing with your pronunciation and articulation.*

SOUND NECKLACE EXERCISE

An interesting method of exploring your own vocalizations and sound-making is to picture the words and phrases of a song as a series of shapes and colours, linked by your breath. Sing the evocative sea shanty *Shanendoah* softly to yourself, and imagine the sounds in this way. The result is not unlike a "necklace" of sounds, shown above.

Your breath is the thread of the necklace and it is vitally important; it must be strong and flexible, and carefully knotted between each bead. Think of these breath-knots as the definitive consonants which give space to your vowel sounds. Just as knotting takes up a surprising amount of thread, the utterance of consonants takes up breath.

Get to know your voice and your articulations intimately by experimenting with various tunes in this way. Use real beads, or make your own vowel-beads from modelling clay or wax. Listen carefully to your sounds, and intuitively shape and reshape the clay until it feels right for the vowel quality you wish to make. Choose a special thread to represent the breath, because it symbolizes the heart of the music as well as the continuity of the necklace.

There is another dimension to the regular steps of the sounds of a musical scale. Inwardly, scales symbolize the human capacity to function happily on various levels, to move freely through the range of life's experiences, navigating by the feelings in the heart. Today, many people have lost touch with their soul's potential range of heartfelt emotions, from kindness to gentle true love, from devotion to all-consuming blind passion. These many nuances form a scale—of emotions. In many systems of medicine, problems stem from blocked or suppressed emotions which originate in a denial of the heart. Your voice can link your conscious and unconscious self, thereby opening your heart to the "scale" of emotions in a powerfully therapeutic manner.

A series of ascending postures accompanies the notes of the familiar Western scale. You can think of these notes and movements as corresponding to stepwise "scales" in your emotions and feelings. This enables you to direct and even manipulate your emotions, by inwardly concentrating on sounds and postures, which reflect an increase or decrease in intensity.

SINGING SCALES EXERCISE

Singing the scale can help to bring together stepwise increments in your emotions, movements, and vocalizations. Try the familiar scale beginning on middle C: *doh ray me fa so la te doh*. Ascend and descend at whatever speed you choose. Complement the notes with actions, as shown below. Make the steps into a dance: miss a note, miss another, and then miss two, as in *doh me so doh*, while omitting the relevant actions. This transforms your scale into an arpeggio, a series of linked notes that form a chord, as when the strings of a chord are plucked in turn on the guitar.

INNER VOICE EXERCISE

This exercise focuses on your pelvic area, which is the centre of your feelings and emotions (see page 118). Lie on the floor, in the first position (below), and follow the movement described, into the second position. Holding this, take a deep breath in; then on your out-breath, open your mouth and let out whatever sound you feel you want to make, but not too loudly. As the sound emerges, lower your pelvis gently back to the floor. When it reaches the floor, let the impact release your voice more fully. Allow the sound of your voice to continue until it stops naturally. Repeat this exercise about six times. The pitch of your voice may change slightly as you do so, indicating that you are releasing emotions trapped in your lower back area.

First position Lie comfortably on the floor, arms loose by your sides. Take six relaxed breaths, then bend your knees and bring the soles of your feet on to the floor (left).

Second position With arms on the floor, lift up your pelvis as far as is comfortable (right). Breathe normally for a few seconds. Take a deep breath in, and lower your pelvis as you release a sound. As your pelvis touches the floor, permit your voice to release the sound more fully.

Inner voice and body posture

Your inner voice is the still, small voice that exists deep within you. When freely released, it pervades and strengthens the sounds of your personality. However, your inner voice can be dominated or suppressed by tensions and blocked emotions in your mind. These tensions are often manifested as areas of muscular contraction or "armour", as described below. You can use your inner voice to increase your awareness of your body, to move into a more harmonious relationship with it, to release emotions, and to develop your creative imagination.

Sound and movement exercises can help you to release your inner voice. Each exercise can be adjusted to focus on a specific part of the body and result in the release of different sounds, reflecting the fact that we hold on to a variety of problems within our bodies, in different areas. An example of such an exercise is described on page 72. You can use this basic approach to explore and release sounds from other regions of your body, by following the relevant body de-armouring exercises on pages 74-77.

The sounds that emerge from your body during these activities are rarely tuneful or musical, or even pleasant to hear. They may seem unusually low- or high-pitched, a reflection of your emotional condition. Do not let this unsettle you. Any sound is fine. You are learning to recognize and rid yourself of negative influences, so that your body and mind become more tuneful and harmonious. This will reflect in your voice and posture.

In these exercises, you should centre your mind on the movements, not on the sound. As you repeat the movements, the pitch of your voice will rise, indicating that tensions and problems are ebbing away.

Body de-armouring

Your body is a home to your habitual emotional attitudes and habitual thoughts. It "holds" and is shaped by these factors. Areas of self-imposed rigidity and tension can

"Every problem exists to be solved.
Every problem waits for the answer to come.
Every problem is a door waiting to be opened."

Olivea Dewhurst-Maddock

develop (see page 47) which affect your posture. These areas symbolize your reluctance either to express or to receive. The process is termed "body armouring". The armoured areas are commonly silent, and all-too-often unrecognized—yet they are signatures of pain, fear, rejection, and shame. Some are rooted in life in the womb; others in infancy and childhood; still others are acquired into body consciousness through adulthood. As they persist and accumulate, these tensions can imperceptibly harden into a sort of shield or shell-like carapace, which is both protective and imprisoning.

The exercises on pages 74-77 are a guide to loosening and freeing the principal areas of restriction in your body. For each part, the possible causes of blocking and armouring are listed; followed by their relationships to body systems, functions, and problems; and associated sound therapies which aid the exercises. Explore each area in turn, or consider if a description relates to your own situation. Try one or a few of the exercises daily, for about fifteen minutes. Such breathing and voice exercises can open up the processes of acceptance and the release of blocked emotions. Remember to begin each exercise with a minute or two of deep breaths, for relaxation.

1

starting pitch. With each bend, make the sound louder, and bring your body lower to the floor (3). This loosens your hips and pelvic area. Finally, lie on the floor and curl into the fetal position (4), and relax like this for a few minutes.

Pelvic area *Stand with your arms out to the side (1). Bend your knees and lower your body (2), saying "ooh!" as you do so. Straighten up, then repeat the bending movement. Do this about 10-20 times, expelling breath and saying "ooh!" each time, beginning on a low note that rises and then falls to the*

2

3

4

1

2

3

Waist and diaphragm area
Punch the air and stamp on the floor (1). Then throw your arms up, and punch the air again as you utter "ooh!" (2).

Do this 20-30 times, stamping with alternate feet. Finally, lie down in the recovery position used by first aiders (3) and relax for a few minutes.

1

2

Belly area (see page 76) Make slow hip swings and circles, like "hula hoop" movements, for 2-3 minutes, saying "ugh!" with each rotation (1). Then relax, lying on your back with knees bent (2).

Pelvic area

Causes of blocking Harsh repression of sexuality, the impression that sex is forbidden or shameful, perhaps compounded by over-insistent toilet-training; rejection of, or conflicting preoccupation with, your pelvic area.

Body relationships Sexual functions; bowel processes; standing and walking, contact with the ground; feelings of security, endurance, and independence. Holding in old traumas, or refusing to acknowledge your instincts.

Sound therapies Try listening to ethnic music with powerful rhythms. Sing while tidying or cleaning, in the garden sweeping leaves or digging, in the lavatory, and when touching the earth with crystals (see page 114).

Waist and diaphragm area

Causes of blocking Repression of personal power; self-control understood as the control of external events, not of yourself; breath-holding, and temper tantrums; rage against apparent injustice; "lost" opportunities and the waste of talent; anger; self-defeating pride.

Body relationships Judgmental attitude and discrimination; health problems such as ulcers, and liver and gall-bladder conditions; holding in resentment or refusing to acknowledge your inner will.

Sound therapies Try listening to choral compositions such as those of George Frederick Handel. Sing near sources of heat

1

such as the log fire, garden bonfire, oven, even the central-heating system. Also, try singing before your mealtimes.

Belly area

Causes of blocking Repression and suppression of feelings and emotions, of your needs, of anger and "gut" reactions that are pushed down; also, being left hungry or made to eat when not hungry; punishment for unacceptable behaviour; memories, often subconscious, that you have left unprocessed, to ferment and become reservoirs of toxicity.
Body relationships Your bodily nutrition, digestion, and elimination; cravings for comfort foods, or the rejection of

Heart and chest area Over cushions and pillows, lie both on your front and back (1).

2

3

Breathe rhythmically and say "aah!", for 1-2 minutes. Then stand and swing your arms to the front and back (above), with an "aah!" for each swing. Relax by lying on your back, arms outstretched (3).

foods as in anorexic dietary disorders; and generally holding in your feelings and refusing to acknowledge your emotional responses (see exercise on page 75).
Sound therapies Try listening to string quartets and music by Maurice Ravel. Sing in the vicinity of water: in the bath or shower, in the rain, and by the sea or swimming pool.

Heart and chest area

Causes of blocking Rejection; the denial of love; fear of loving; repression of tenderness; loneliness and lack of physical contact; fear disguised as self-assertion or defeat; heartache; hard-heartedness or heartlessness.
Body relationships Problems communicating with others;

Throat area Tilt your head from side to side, and from front to back, saying "argh!" with each motion, for two minutes. Shrug your shoulders hard, saying "ayh!" each time. Relax curled up into a ball (below).*

holding in heartbreak or refusing to acknowledge love; heart and lung conditions such as bronchitis or asthma.

Sound therapies Try listening to *The Lark Ascending* by Ralph Vaughan Williams, and similar light, soaring pieces. Sing while out of doors and in touch with the wind, while facing the wind, or walking backward into the wind, on hilltops, among trees.

Throat area

Causes of blocking Unusually traumatic birth; experience of suffocation or choking; feelings that are denied expression; thick mucus or catarrh; denial of beauty; sexual frustration; shock and grief.

Body relationships Attention and concentration factors; voice and hearing conditions; holding in feelings of restriction or refusing to acknowledge the value of creativity.

Sound therapies Try listening to Wolfgang Amadeus Mozart's *Eine Kleine Nacht Musik* and John Taverner's *The Protecting Veil*. Sing during creative recreations such as writing, reading, painting, sewing, and sculpting.

Jaw area *(see page 78) Spend a few minutes exercising and even contorting your face and mouth: yawn, gnash, puff cheeks, blow hard, suck in cheeks, stretch mouth and lips, poke out tongue. Feel the mobility and loosening effects. Relax in the kneeling prayer position (above).*

3

Eye area *(see page 78) Move and contort your face. Squint, roll, and widen your eyes. Place your hands on the sides of your head, say "eeh!" loudly, and feel the vibrations (1). Hold your forehead and chin, and do the same (2). After a few minutes, relax and assume the easy meditation pose (3).*

1

2

Jaw area

Causes of blocking Problems in eating, speech difficulties, traumatic teething when young; the denial of comfort; not being allowed to "speak out"; learning to survive by adopting faked helplessness or defiance; pressures to mature very early or very late.

Body relationships Tongue, teeth, lips, and mouth; verbalization; continuing colds and respiratory infections; migraine; holding in aggression (see exercise on page 77).

Sound therapies Try listening to Samuel Barber's *Adagio for Strings*. Share your auditory experiences by singing to someone, or with someone; participate in group singing.

Eye area

Causes of blocking Fear of the dark; being forced to look at things or not being allowed to "see" what is there; forced or pressurized intellectual development; buying affections through achievements; a need to succeed and be first, the "top dog" in all matters.

Body relationships Sight and general muscular coordination;

SOUND-RELEASE EXERCISE

If you have trouble releasing sounds and letting them flow from deep within you, especially when involved in fairly complex activities such as those described on pages 74–77, try this exercise first (see also page 45).

Stand up straight, arms hanging loose by your sides. Drop into a forward bend at your waist, breathing out, and keeping your legs straight. As you breathe in, stand straight again. Bring your arms up and around in an arc, taking them horizontally to your sides, and then over your head, to join your palms there. Hold the breath for as long as is comfortable. As you release it, reverse the movements by bringing your arms down to your sides, lean forward, and straighten again. Let your sound out as you go forward. This helps you to coordinate movement and vocalization.

academic ability; headaches, mental stress, and fatigue, and psychosomatic diseases; very distorted, obsessive, or fanatical views; holding in painful realizations or refusing to accept and acknowledge perceptions (see exercise on page 77).
Sound therapies Try listening to *Fantasia on a Theme of Thomas Tallis* by Ralph Vaughan Williams. Sing to and into the darkness and the void: to the night sky, to the moon and the stars, and to the darkening dusk.

Self-exploration and musical instruments

"See deep enough and you see musically; the heart of nature being everywhere music, if you can only reach it."

Thomas Carlyle

Let a musical instrument help you in your journey of self-exploration and personal discovery. An instrument, rather than your voice, gives you another way to produce sounds that sing in harmony with your soul. Be guided by your instincts and intuitions in the type of instrument you select, following the strands of your personality as well as your proficiency at playing.

In many cultures, musical instruments are treasured as the "voices" by which nature can be imitated and charmed, pacified and roused. Instruments are the mouthpieces through which the gods can speak and sing. Music-making, however imperfect, is a therapeutic activity, and a source of deep satisfaction.

There are no short-cuts to the mastery of a musical instrument. The essential ingredients are time, instruction, and the habit of practice. But undertaking such a musical apprenticeship is an investment that will bring rewards for a lifetime. Once you acquire a reasonable standard of technical skill, you may wish to gain admission to a band or orchestra, with its potential for rich musical experiences and friendships based on a shared enthusiasm.

Exploring instruments

If you feel drawn to the idea, explore the possibility of learning some basic technique and having "hands-on" experience, before committing yourself to a long course of tuition or the financial outlay of buying an instrument. There are amateur music groups and bands in most areas,

LISTENING EXERCISE

If you are unsure about making and playing musical instruments, this meditative exercise may help to encourage your interest and enhance your listening abilities.

Listen to a recording of string music, preferably in the baroque or classical style. Imagine yourself back in the seventeenth or eighteenth century, in the workshop of a musical instrument-maker. You are his apprentice, and you have come to know all the careful planning, the choice of woods, the months of work, the disappointments, the mistakes, the revisions, and the endless patience of the master craftsman. You hold the tools, tend the fire, boil up the glue, run about the narrow streets of the town with messages. Each day, you sweep up the wood shavings that cover the workshop floor. You see the instrument taking shape, being smoothed and varnished, pitched and strung; every detail is perfected. At last, the slow and exacting work is finished. You share your master's pride when the instrument is placed into the hands of a great performer. Listen as the music brings the instrument to life.

Now play the recording through again. Listen!

and the members are usually only too pleased to help. Do not feel that you have been let down if your first choice of instrument or band proves unsuccessful. Keep your options open; attend as many live performances as you can; talk to instrumentalists; ask questions; look for information in libraries and music shops; find out as much as possible about the instruments to which you are attracted; and be adventurous and flexible.

Comparatively inexpensive "educational" instruments, common in schools and other teaching establishments, can be played with no less musicianship and artistry than their more costly and exotic orchestral cousins. Examine and explore the sounds and potentialities of recorders, chime bars, glockenspiels, auto-harps, xylophones, bird-callers, tin whistles, tambourines, and finger cymbals. Try the intriguing wealth of traditional and ethnic instruments now available from all parts of the world.

Simplest of all are instruments made at home from every-day objects and easily-obtained materials. Making bamboo pipes is not difficult, and the resulting flute-like tone is beautifully sweet and mellow. Curve a sheet of strong card into a half cylinder, cut notches in the short ends, and string it with elastic for a zither. Making instruments is fun, and a way of exploring the principles of pitch and resonance. Music is not the exclusive prerogative of the young, or the exceptionally gifted. It is for everyone. Remember: it is never too late to begin something wonderful!

Milk bottles, filled with water to different levels, produce various notes, and you can play them like a xylophone. Tune the notes by adding or pouring away water. Saucepans or clay flower pots, arranged in order of size, can also become splendid xylophones or marimbas.

81

Science in our modern age has seen a great movement toward the unity of Nature. Physicists seek the secrets of quarks and the fundamental particles of matter, and the key to the grand unifying theory which brings together electro-magnetism, gravity, and other forces of nature. Cosmologists look back to the beginning, to the Big Bang, when time, matter, and energy were one. And they look forward to the ultimate unification, the so-called Big Crunch.

Running parallel to these researches is our own search for unification: a growing urgency in the human consciousness as we strive for meaning, for healing, for holistic living, and for a spirituality that can encompass religious and/or philo-sophical diversity. This search leads to meditation, for through meditation, we can achieve the unification of our consciousness with nature, our planet, and ultimately, the Universe. The following pages are a guide to the use of various sounds and music for meditation. They aim to help you make the vital connections, so that you can experience the point at which you are at one with the Universe.

Music and mantras

The ultimate value of music in meditation is that it leads you to a reality beyond itself: the "silence" from which it arises, and to which it returns. The practice of music requires an attention, a listening, which leads your consciousness to the threshold of unification—where your normal limitations of perception can be transcended, however briefly.

Speaking or singing mantras (see page 92) is an ancient and well-proven method of achieving this liberation of awareness—in the most simple, even unlikely, way. Mantras are uniquely simplified utterances; quintessential music; a bridge between individual voices and the primordial sound of silence; the Aum (OM). The discipline of simplicity is release: let go of the poverty of your earthly being and allow your spirit to gain admission to the kingdom of unity.

Begin by contemplating natural sounds: the sea, a moun-tain stream, wind, rainfall, bird song, trees and animals, your

"All things by immortal power, Near or far, Hiddenly, To each other linked are.
Thou can'st not stir a flower Without troubling of a star."
Francis Thompson

Moving water produces endless, soothing sounds, from the restful murmur of waves on the beach, to the gush of a mountainside waterfall. Immerse yourself in the watery world as an aid to contemplation.

footsteps in a walking meditation, your body's inner sounds, especially the sound of your breathing. As you listen, become aware that every natural sound, every conscious utterance, every note you sing, can be understood on four levels, each moving further from our familiar physical world with its conscious mental perceptions.

First, as an audible sound, the "physical" result transmitted to your ears, from molecular vibrations and impacts in every degree of force and refinement.

The Sanskrit symbol for the Aum (OM)—sometimes called "the first mantra". The long lower curve represents the dream state, the upper left curve is the waking state, and the central curve projecting to the right is the deep, dreamless sleep between them. The crescent on the upper right symbolizes the veil of illusion, maya, and the dot beyond it is the transcendental state.

Second, as the feelings and the thoughts within and behind the sounds. The singer must initially "sing" to express her or his thoughts in the mind, before the physical voice can ring true.

Third, as the "sonic seeds" from which grow the roots and branches of music and language. Sounds are the seeds of an entire tree that grows into leaf, and whose countless leaves each represent one element of vocal and verbal expansion in a spoken language or a musical tradition. The seeds contain the potential of communication and understanding, since when the tree flowers it bears the fruits which themselves carry seeds. In this way, new languages and new forms of music appear, and evolve through time. The tree symbol appears in many traditions, as the World Tree, the Tree of Life, and the Tree of Knowledge.

Fourth, as the *Anahata* or universal heart (see opposite)— sounds unheard and unmade, from which the whole symphony of creation is born. At this last stage of refinement, sound is said to be united with light, in the primordial radiance of the Word, the Aum (OM). Yet fragments of the *Anahata*—the most subtle and sacred of sounds—can be realized inwardly by some people, as though "heard" deep within the soul or spirit. These inner sounds are experienced by mystics and sensitives, who liken them to "thunder, tinkling bells, flute music, or the humming of bees" yet with a delicacy and beauty beyond all earthly sound.

Meditation develops access to fragments of the *Anahata*. If you hear such "inaudible sounds", you will almost certainly know, and you will probably not need to talk about the experience. There is no point in trying to force your consciousness to hear them, or try to "make" them happen.

There is only one channel by which these subtle sounds can manifest themselves. This is by opening your heart so

HEART SOUND EXERCISE

To tune into the sounds of your heart, hum or sing a vowel sound such as "ooo". Begin at a pitch below middle C. Slowly and smoothly, glide your voice upward, rather like a musical siren. Pause and breathe as necessary, and do not hurry. As the sound rises in pitch, imagine that it is also rising up your spinal column, from its base. At certain points along the musical "slide", you may sense a reaction: a subtle feeling of pressure, added resonance, heat or cold, or a slight quivering of your breath. The first point of sensitivity may well be one of the special spinal centres of energy with spiritual connections, called Chakras (see page 118). From here, work more slowly to find notes for other Chakras. Listen, sing, and feel with great care and attention in your spine, until you reach and recognize the vibration of your *Anahata* Chakra or heart centre, in the centre of your chest.

Stay with this note for a time and experience the inner sensations. This is the pitch to which you should return, to establish a "bridge" between your physical, day-to-day world and the greater cosmos, which is unknowable in its totality. It is also the centre from which you can expand your voice to a richer, more meaningful expression. The pitch is known as the "cardiac tone" in some Eastern traditions. When the note feels secure, proceed in the same way through the higher pitches, and the higher Chakra centres of your spine. Sing gently; do not push or force. Imagine the sounds below the cardiac tone rising from the forces and elements of Gaia's earth, and those above coming from the cosmos of spiritual energies. Both streams meet in your heart, and from there, radiate out as your song.

that your heart and soul, not your ears and mind, listen for the fragments and the echoes of the inaudible, but not undetectable, *Anahata* sounds.

Approaching mantras

Every true mantra has a melodic form uniquely its own—its own Chladni figure or Jenny image (see page 30). This melodic form has been present since ancient times. Accumulated energy resides in the mantric sound, which through age and repetition gathers a "life of its own". The energy should help to carry you, as a beginner, through the early stages of mantric discipline. Examples of mantras are on pages 92-93. Gradually the mantra becomes your respected friend, a pillar of strength to support your resolve.

How have mantras passed through time? Many venerable and inspired mantras were revealed to mystics and visionaries while immersed in the deepest meditation. Something of their achievement and virtue is transferred by the sound, into the heart of the devotee. These sacred sounds are believed to descend via the masters of wisdom, from the subtle realms of the *Anahata*; and they have remained a consecrated means of expansion and ascent for students of subsequent generations. Yet in a sense, mantras are timeless: they are continually forgotten and rediscovered, they are at once old and new, and their source, power, and purpose belong to eternity. From traditional Buddhist chants to the waves of sincere devotion rising from your own heart into song—these are all mantric filaments in the thread of tradition, from which the seamless robe of unity is woven.

The study and practice of mantras is the task of a lifetime. If you are drawn to meditation and this area of sound therapy, it is best to receive instruction from a teacher of the mantric path. Remember: make haste slowly, and when the pupil is ready, the teacher will appear.

Mantras and "Words of Power"

Mantras are often linked to the concept of "Words of Power". Through history such special sounds have been

HISTORICAL DEVOTION TO MANTRAS AND MEDITATION

Many physical objects have been used as aids to mantras and prayers for healing. Knotted threads, fringes, or small pebbles were used for counting the number of mantric repetitions. Desert hermits and Celtic monks hauled man-sized rocks from one location to another and assembled them for each devout series of repetitions. Since these spiritual athletes thought nothing of singing at several sites throughout the night, we can only marvel at their zeal as the huge stone piles were dismantled, moved, and rebuilt.

Chanting is a central feature in the ancient religions of East and West, Old World and New. This Buddhist monk is taking part in a peace ceremony.

87

viewed as sonic formulae which have the power to transmute matter, reverse natural processes, even materialize and
de-materialize objects, and precipitate events. But the right
use of such "sound dynamite" is far removed from our
earthly existence. It can be exercised only by beings who are
living embodiments of love, who no longer function in
terms of personal gain or advantage. Such beings have no
need to prove anything; they want nothing. Nature yields in
reverence to them, for they are love incarnate.

Nearer our own planes of existence, we may only hope
that our own "words of power" have the energies to transmute fear into courage, confusion into wisdom, anxiety into
trust, and sorrow into joy.

Chanting

Chanting is rapidly growing in popularity as a tranquillizing
and "battery-recharging" activity, providing the opportunity
for spiritual experience and a unity with the cosmos. Sacred
songs, psalms, mantras, and hymns have long been intoned
as a source of solace and inspiration. Also, chanting techniques such as overtone chanting (see opposite), coupled
with meditation, have therapeutic powers by establishing
and maintaining the tuneful harmony between human and
heavenly existence.

The *Vedas*, the oldest of the sacred texts of India, express
these concepts in a religious language that would be difficult
for most modern Westerners to follow. The loose translation
given here attempts to summarize the four stages of chanting, while retaining a flavour of the original.

First, there is silence and formlessness.

Second, the creative Word precipitates the cosmos, and
the interaction of all energies.

Third, your individual consciousness hears the Word,
recognizes it, and returns the separated parts to the whole,
by singing the music in a "sacrifice" of song.

Fourth, you reach fulfilment within reunification.

Overtone chanting

The vocal and therapeutic meditation of overtone chanting had long been a secretive, esoteric tradition. During the past thirty years, dedicated practitioners and teachers in Europe and the United States have made it more generally available.

Overtones exist in every vocal sound. They are sets of harmonic frequencies related to the main pitch, or note, of the voice (see page 17). It is helpful to picture them as the petals of a flower, closed and folded inward. Overtone chanting aims to open the flower and reveal the true beauty, complexity, and delicacy of the bloom. It is truly amazing to hear the constituent elements of the voice opened out, clearly and separately, with the sets of overtones being produced simultaneously.

Overtone chanting is a centuries-old technique, usually practised in a religious or ritual context, across the world: in Tibet, Siberia, Mongolia, and Northern India; in Buddhist communities in China and Japan; in the Andes of South America; in Europe, in Bulgaria and Romania; and in Central Africa. Traces of the technique remain in Spanish flamenco music, itself of Indian origin. Clues suggest that overtones were known in medieval monasteries and convents, where highly decorative group singing may have combined with the resonance of ecclesiastical architecture to reveal astounding harmonics, to which the human ear is especially sensitive.

Overtone chanting offers therapeutic possibilities, inner stillness and security, enhanced sensitivity to outer sounds, and a profound, meditative pathway to wisdom. But such a powerful technique is not easily acquired. No amount of formal training or coaching can capture overtones or guarantee their manifestation. Each meditational exploration of these "sounds within sound" is unique; a new and wholly uncertain adventure; a journey into inner space and universal law. If you are attracted to the idea of learning about overtone chanting, it is wise to begin by seeking out a teacher, a group or class, where you can receive practical and individual instruction. You will be able to hear and

"A good word is a Divine Name, recalled, remembered, and invoked in an upward aspiration toward the Truth.
It is like a tree, firmly rooted in the Zikr—the invocation, prayer, or mantram.
Like branches, the tremendous meaning of the invocation grows upward through the Universe; like rich fruit is the reality of the harvest it provides."

Abu Bakr Siraj al-Din

Note	C	D	E
Sense	Smell	Taste	Sight
Body parts	Bones, muscles of lower back, sciatic nerve, hips, buttocks, lower bowel, legs, ankles, feet, prostate gland, blood hemoglobin; corrects loss of egocentricity	Body fluids, kidneys and bladder, lymphatic system, reproductive system, fat deposits, skin; links physical and mental energies	Nerves and muscular energies, liver and intestines, solar plexus, spleen, kidneys, cellular repair; stimulates intellectual activity
Effective therapy for	Poor circulation, iron deficiency anemia and other blood disorders, paralysis, swollen ankles and cold feet, lumbago, stiff joints, constipation or diarrhoea, urinary difficulties, melancholia	Asthma, bronchitis, gout, gallstones, obesity, purification and removal of toxins and poisons, lethargy and apathy	Constipation, indigestion, flatulence, liver and gastrointestinal disorders, coughs, headaches, poor skin condition, sluggishness, boredom, headaches
Reflexed to	Colon, neck, knees, nose	Breasts, reproductive organs, perineal floor, feet, tongue	Head, eyes, solar plexus, umbilical area, thighs

MUSICAL NOTES AND THEIR THERAPEUTIC APPLICATIONS

This chart shows the links between specific notes and the body's senses and systems. To improve functioning of the specified part of your body, sing your chants and mantras in the relevant notes, and expose yourself to sounds and music based on these notes.

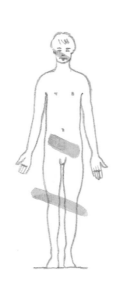  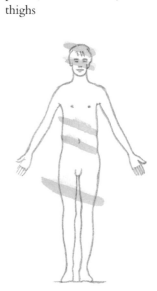

F	G	A	B
Touch, feeling	Hearing	Intuition	--
Heart and lungs, shoulders, arms, hands, pituitary and other hormone glands, immune system, automatic processes such as sweating; a natural antiseptic and emotionally soothing to all areas	Throat and neck, blood and circulation, spine and nervous system, metabolism and temperature control, ears, immune system, tissue renewal; stimulates extraversion	All the senses, muscular responses and control and coordination, pain and pain control, blood disorders	Blood and fluid balance of potassium and sodium, calcium and phosphorus, iron, iodine and other minerals, spleen stimulant; aid to meditation
Hay fever and allergies, head colds, trauma and shock, colic, exhaustion, ulcers, sleeplessness, irritability, high blood pressure, back pains, dry skin,	Laryngitis, tonsillitis and throat infections, headaches, eye problems, skin disorders and itching, vomiting, muscular spasms, period pains, fevers; centres attention and calms	All nervous ailments, convulsions, obsessions, balance disorders, excessive bleeding, breathing difficulties, swellings and palsy, shingles; sedative effects	Neuralgia, cramps and inflammatory pains, glandular imbalance, immune deficiencies, vitamin processing problems, goitre, nervous disorders; restores self-respect
Kidneys and suprarenal glands, shoulders, chest, colon, calves, ankles	Reproductive system, saliva, hair	Sacrum (base of spine)	Whole body

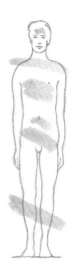

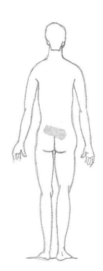
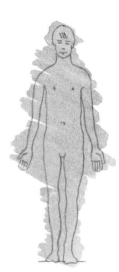

SELECTED MANTRAS

BUDDHIST MANTRAS

Buddhist mantras are associated with mandalas—images of the cosmos, prayer wheels and beads, and counters. Repeating the mantra 108 times is auspicious because of the numbers: 1 is The Absolute, 0 is The Cosmos, and 8 is Infinity.

Gate, Gate, Paragate, Paramsagate Bodhi Svaha *Gone, gone, gone to the other shore, safely passed to that other shore, Enlightened One*

Namo Buddya, Namo Dharmaya, Namo Snaghaya *I go to the Buddha for refuge, I go to the Dharma for refuge, I go to the Sangha for refuge*

Bhagavan Sarva Tathagatha *Blest be all ye Buddhas!*

Om Ah Hum *The Trinity of Power: Creation, Maintenance, Dissolution*

Om Tare Tutare Ture Swaha *Hail to Tara*

Namo Amitabha *I go to the Buddha for Light*

Om Mani Padme Hum *Hail to the Jewel in the Lotus*

SIKH MANTRA

Eck Ong Kar Sat Nam Siri Wha Guru *The Supreme is one, His names are many*

HINDU MANTRAS

Tat Tuam Asi *Thou art that*

So ham *That I am*

Hare Krishna *Hail to Krishna*

Hare Rama *Hail to Rama*

Om Namah Sivaya *Om Reverence to Shiva*

Shanti Shanti *Peace Peace*

These mantras have particular healing associations:

Hrim *Hreeemmm......* Throat area

Hrum *Hrooommm......* Liver, spleen

Hraim *Hraheemmm......* Kidneys, diuretic

Hraum *Hrowmmm.....* Organs of elimination

Hra *Hrah.....* Heart and chest

ISLAMIC MANTRAS

Allah, Allah *God, God*

La Ilaha Illa'llah *There is no God but one God*

Insha Allah *If God wills*

Ya—Salaam *God the source of Peace*

An—Nur *God, the Light*

JEWISH MANTRAS

Adonai *Lord*

Shalom *Peace*

Ehyeh Asher Ehyeh *I am that I am*

Qadosh, Quadosh, Quadosh, Adonai Tzeba'oth *Holy, Holy, Holy Lord of Hosts*

Barukh Ata Adonai *Blessed is the Lord*

Eli, Eli, Elu *My God, My God, My God*

CHRISTIAN MANTRAS

Lord Jesus Christ, Son of God, Have Mercy on us

Kyrie Eleison, Christe Eleison, Kyrie Eleison *Lord have mercy, Christ have mercy, Lord have mercy*

Laudamus Te *We praise Thee*

Alleluia!

Maranatha *Come, Lord*

Holy, Holy, Holy

En Emoi Christus *Christ in me*

Ave Maria *Hail Mary*

SAI BABA MANTRAS

Om, Sai, Ram

Satya Dharma Shanti Prema *Truth, The Path, Peace, Love*

SUFI MANTRAS

Hu E-haiy *God the living*

Hu—La *...the Word is the mirror wherein the Divine reverberates outwardly, through sound the world will be reabsorbed. The word is both sound and light, for light is the meaning of the word!*

CELTIC MANTRAS

Awn *Ah...ooh...nn...* A Celtic Aum

Aoh Eeh Ooh *Ancient Celtic tradition describes the revelation of the Word to the "Son of the Three Shouts" (a Seer) in this way:* God spoke His name and light was born; In the light was life—including humanity. The Seer perceived three columns—Sound, Light, Form—yet the three were one. The Son of the Three Shouts understood that, by hearing the voices and seeing the Form, mankind could know all creatures. From the three columns came the "Three Shouts" or sacred vowels, and their written symbols.

Let the Light Shine *A healing prayer of the White Eagle Lodge*

observe other "overtones" at work, and share your experiences. (The names of relevant organizations are listed on page 122.) In the meantime, if you wish to experiment by yourself with these very special sounds for meditation, the guidelines below and on page 94 may help. But much remains to be re-discovered. Approach the topic without hurry, and without the ambition to be extraordinary.

Sounds of the planet and the Universe

The universe is full of light, cosmic rays, and many other forms of radiations and waves, which our modern telescopes can interpret and transform into sounds for our ears. These

PREPARATORY OVERTONE EXERCISE

Real spirituality in music depends upon its resonance—in other words, its harmonics. You can gain initial familiarity with this from the following exercise. Take a short phrase or single word. As you intone or chant it, slow down your processes of utterance as much as possible. Observe every detail: the subtle flow of movements in your larynx and mouth, and the stream of your breath. When you need to inhale, try to do so without moving any muscles in your face and mouth and larynx, and take up the sound exactly where you "left off".

Your mouth, throat, the sinuses, windpipe, and lungs are resonant spaces that all contribute to the "shaping" of vowel sounds, initiated by the pressure of your breath in your larynx. Concentrate your attention upon these shapes, these inner forms. Focus on their qualities, since you should try to become liberated from the insistent rush of verbal quantities which is our normal pattern of speech. This is why the "slowing down" is essential. Give yourself time to listen. Remember that harmonics are generated by elegant proportional relationships (see page 23). In singing overtones, you are recovering and demonstrating these proportions in your own resonant spaces.

OVERTONE EXERCISES

The dancer Relax your tongue by extending it outward and inward, curling the sides and the tip, and rolling it back so that its underside touches the ridge at the back of the roof of your mouth. In Indian singing, the tongue is called "the dancer", and the mouth is "the theatre" in which the dancer performs. Progress to making open vowel sounds such as "ooo" and "aaa" as you practise the tongue movements.

The stage Move your lower jaw, the "stage" for your oral theatre, in all directions: up and down, side to side, forward and back. Do not force the movements. Relax for a moment, then allow your jaw to "fall", opening your mouth to its greatest natural extent. Again, no stretching. Just let go! This exercise loosens your mouth for …

The theatre With your jaw, neck, throat, and lips all relaxed, breathe without tension. Open your mouth—inside as well as outside—and sing the "aaa" vowel, at a pitch in the middle of your voice's range. Working very slowly, without pushing, move your tongue and mouth cavity through the vowel sequence: "ah, oh, oo, ayh, ee, ah, oh, oo, ayh, ee" and so on, repeating these over a minute or two. Pay particular attention to the vibrations and resonances in your nasal passages at each stage. With practice, the overtones will become audible. Remember to be patient with yourself. During the exercise, time will fly, and your mind will be diverted and emerge relaxed.

radio-astronomy researches have revealed an orchestral variety of "sounds" originating from the Earth itself, from our planetary neighbours in the Solar System, from the Sun at the centre of the system, and also from mysterious sources of gigantic power, deep in space. Transmuted into sounds, they produce rhythmic patterns that crackle, hiss, and hum; deep planetary "sighs" and drummings; clock-like ticks and random bursts of clicks; regular pulses from pulsars and

Earth hangs in apparent silence in the void of space. Yet there is no true emptiness. Space is filled with waves of light and other forms of natural radiation. Like music and the planet itself, these conform to universal laws of harmony and proportion.

quasars; the sounds of the solar wind, cosmic tides and colliding star systems, and the voices of stars passing through their lives, from contracting whorls of gas and dust, to expanding red giants and dying white dwarfs.

Our Sun emits energies whose frequencies bear musical relationships in terms of fundamental notes, harmonics, and overtones—eighty harmonies so far identified, in cycles running from two to eight minutes. Changes of frequency, and the crescendos of power transmitted by sunspots and solar flares, have profound effects on terrestrial life. On our planet itself, seismographs recording the shock waves of earthquakes have shown that Earth "rings" like a great bell when struck by an earthquake, at frequencies with 53.1-minute and 54.7-minute cycles. These, and many other calculations, demonstrate the wide range of connections between sound, music, and the movements and energies of the stars and planets.

Instruments in meditation

You can use any instrument—ethnic, modern, exotic, or familiar—as an aid to meditation, once its inner significance is recognized. The inner significance lies in the symbolic relationships between music and the unfolding levels or planes of the human psyche. The secrets of musical ratio and harmony, order and proportion, are hidden in the higher or spiritual self; the secrets of rhythm are hidden in flesh, bone, sinew, and blood, and in birth, procreation, and death. The musician who lives from the central core, with his or her heart as an inexhaustible well of courage, finally gains (often at great expense) the precious token of god-like power, by overcoming the forces of separation and fragmentation—in other words, one who understands music as a sacred mystery is a healer.

Musical instruments and their symbolism

In meditation, as in life itself, there are no inherently sacred or profane instruments. Thus, if you wish to incorporate music and instruments into your meditations, consider the

MYSTERIUM TREMENS

On the next clear night, go out and look at the stars. Contemplate the music you cannot hear: patterns of light etched across time, older than the Earth under your feet. Ashes and fire.

But no alien Universe, empty and strange. No! No! Your seeing eye, and all the precious dust of blood and nerve and limb; of crystal, tree, and bird—is star dust. And in your seething brain, and your restless heart, new stars are born from incandescent song.

"The growth of human character is as the tuning of a lute. If the strings are too slack, there is no music. If they are too taut, they break."

Hindu proverb

instrument which you feel calls to your inner attention. This could be anything from a mighty cathedral organ, to the tiny bells of a *sistrum* (a temple instrument of Ancient Egypt, still used in Ethiopia and Mexico). The relevance of an instrument depends on its effect in facilitating your meditations, which in turn depends on your own intuitions and instincts. These can only be revealed and identified by experiencing the sounds.

Percussion instruments produce music by impact, symbolizing rhythmic vitality. They present an almost endless variety of forms, and many are used in worship and meditation. They include drums of all sizes and shapes, made from all manner of materials; drums pitched in "families"; and shamanist drums and tambourines. In Tibet skull-drums, together with bone–flutes, form part of the insignia of the revered Geshe or Lama-teacher (spiritual leader).

Bells and gongs also figure greatly in meditation. Many religions employ peals of bells to regather the wandering thoughts of the faithful, and recall consciousness to the centre, while demonstrating the radiant nature of sound. Bells were sacred in Celtic Christendom, and those carried by the saints are still treasured. Bells of all sizes, including those that ring out to celebrate freedom, or to solemnize occasions of communal joy or sorrow, are said to purify the surrounding atmosphere of negative energies and emotional debris. Oriental singing bowls, especially those from Tibet, are made from seven "holy" metals and are extraordinarily vibrant, as are meditation gongs from Burma, and Chinese temple bells. Small finger cymbals guide the attention of the meditator to a concentrated "inwardness". Try to experience their effects by following their sound to the very edge of inaudibility.

Think of flutes as representing a simplified human spine— the Chakra (page 118) marked by finger holes. Just as a snake rises in response to the snake charmer's tune, the energies slumbering in the base of the spine rise through their spinal channels in response to the music of "heaven"— the Flute of Shiva. Some wind instruments, such as the

97

Australian aboriginal *didjeridu*, require "circular" breathing, in which the player breathes in and out at the same time. The mouth and nasal cavities are used as reservoirs of air, while the airflows are adjacent. Great concentration, and a deep awareness of the breathing process, are required while mastering this technique.

Before farmers drained the land for crops and pastures, huge reed beds covered low-lying areas in many continents. It was from reed stems that the Pipes of Pan were made. These are the musical ancestors of the church pipe organ, which is still the central instrument of religious centres and meditations, in great cathedrals and places of worship throughout the Western world.

Animal horns, and their metal equivalents in the modern brass section, are ageless symbols of wisdom and authority, from the Jewish ram's-horn *shofar*, to the five-metre Tibetan "Alpenhorn", the *ragdung*. Brass instruments are a musical link with the Earth, and demonstrate the harmonious use of metals forged with the power of fire, extracted from the rocky ores beneath our feet.

Harps were sacred to the Chaldeans, the Egyptians, the Hebrews, the Celts, and the indigenous peoples of South America. The Chinese *cheng*, and other zither-like instruments of the same family, have long been associated with piety and meditation. In the Indian subcontinent, the *sitar* and the *vina* accompany meditative chanting.

Perhaps the most ethereal instrument of all is the Aeolian harp. Traditionally the first of these was the Lyre of Orpheus, which, long after his death, continued to play—touched by the sorrowing winds of heaven (see page 52). Revived by Athanasius Kircher in the seventeenth century, Aeolian harps became immensely popular in the mid nineteenth century. Samuel Taylor Coleridge had such an instrument hung on his window, which may well have inspired these lines: "And what if all of animated nature be but organic harps diversely framed, That tremble into thought as o'er them sweeps plastic and vast, One intellectual breeze, At once the soul of each, and God of all."

"A light in sound, sound-like power in light,
Rhythm in all thought, and joyance everywhere.
... Methinks it should have been impossible,
Not to love all things in a world so filled,
Where the breeze warbles, and the mute still air,
Is music slumbering on her instrument ..."

Samuel Taylor Coleridge

In Greek mythology, Pan was a god of nature, shepherds and their flocks, hunters, wildlife, and fertility. He fashioned reeds into a shepherd's pipe. Variations on the Pipes of Pan occur in many cultures, such as the bamboo pipes played by this South American Indian.

Meditation, sound, and movement

All existence is movement, and living harmoniously within the whole is the Dance of Life, into which you are continuously invited. Your body, mind, and emotions comprise a musical instrument for dancing. In the dance, the inner parts of your spiritual self move as one, united and harmonized with the physical world. Dance, therefore, can be both sacred and healing. In the words of T S Eliot: "The darkness shall be the light, and the stillness, the dancing."

Where you dance is your stage, your space, where the patterns of your life and consciousness can be freely expressed and shared. Movement exercises help you to become increasingly aware of space as a living reality, as important as the objects for which it is the context. The sounds or music that you choose, and the measure of access you have to your own feelings and energies, will determine

99

DANCE TO MUSIC EXERCISE

Select music which is meaningful to you. If you have an instrumentalist friend who can accompany you and improvize, so much the better.

Stand for a moment or two, poised and relaxed. Listen to the music, feel its rhythm. Begin to move and dance, but initially using only your feet. Once your feet have picked up the rhythm, gradually extend movement into your legs, then your knees, up to your hips and body, into arms and hands, then finally up to your neck and head. Try to include every part of yourself in the dance. Enjoy the music, not only with your ears, but with your bones and muscles, with your blood and nerves. Do not hurry. When you feel ready to complete the exercise, close down each area in turn, in reverse order from head to feet, and resume stillness as the music is overtaken by silence.

Which areas of your body "danced" most easily? Did parts of you want to go on dancing? Did you feel the music all the way through the exercise? Answer such questions and focus on total bodily involvement, and you may succeed in being in touch with yourself, and experiencing the coordination and flexibility that are the purpose of the exercise.

how you dance. Meditate on your hopes, joys, sorrows, and dreams—the disciplines by which you strengthen, refine, and perfect your body.

The content of your meditative dance will be the amount of life, uncluttered by distractions, that flows clearly and generously through your every moment and movement. With such understanding, the simplest movements can be a dance to express and transfer physical, emotional, and mental attitudes. The attention you give to your physical health and inner wellbeing reflects your intention to live in this world, and in this present moment, with full-blooded vitality and awareness.

Repetitive movements, like repetitive chants, can bring on trance-like states. Rapid whirling motions are practised by the dervishes (wandering holy men) of certain Islamic communities.

Your body, mind, and spirit continually interact with each other, to produce your overall state of health. Diseases and malfunctions are the result of a cycle of cause and effect, in which a problem in one or more of these spheres—body, mind, and spirit—feeds back to affect the others. The basic rationale of any therapy, including sound therapy, is to intervene and break the cycle, thereby allowing you to re-establish a more balanced pattern and linkage between your physical body, your mental and emotional faculties, and your spirit. This chapter explores the different methods of cycle-breaking, using both the voice, and also sounds from a variety of sources.

The voice in sickness and in health

As described in Chapter Two, the voice reveals much about a person's physical, emotional, and mental wellbeing. By listening to the voices of others, and by objectively tuning into the nature of your own voice, you can find out more about many aspects of health.

Counselling a person has been described as "the art of listening with love". It not only serves to ease suffering; it can bring positive benefits and open the door for the healing process. The counsellor listens to the individual words and their meanings and context; to the subtle layering of implications and associations behind the words and between the lines; to the non-verbal utterances such as sighs and sobs; and to the voice itself—its pitch and tonal qualities, its rhythm and pace, and the gaps and silences between the sounds. In addition, the alert counsellor also takes into account posture and body language, as well as those less explainable nuances of perception which we call intuition and instinct.

Thus the nature of the voice can help to identify and diagnose problems, which is itself the start of the healing process. The table on page 105 shows some of the many links between voice characteristics and physical or mental problems. You can obtain similar pointers to problems not only from the characteristic sound of the voice itself, but

> ### THE HEALTHY VOICE
>
> Your voice reflects your whole health—physical, mental, emotional, and spiritual. The hallmarks of a healthy voice are versatility, sensitivity, warmth, and purity of tone: clear, bright, and open, with no hint of forcing or straining. Above all, the healthy voice possesses vitality—the abundance of vital energy that can triumph over hardship, disappointment, and pain.

Expressive instruments such as the violin are wonderful outlets for feelings and emotions which may otherwise accumulate, with negative effects on whole health.

also from the health of the voice-producing organs. For example, an endless succession of sore throats may be the result of ongoing conflict in a close relationship, even if the disharmony is repressed and vehemently denied.

For those who truly listen with careful attention, the voice can also give insights into how we cope with different stages in life and the processes of development and maturation. The fear of maturity and the emotional demands and responsibilities of adult life is revealed by a "childish" voice and babyish "ba-ba" articulation that can persist into middle age. The husky, breathless "little girl" voice is a characteristic of the predatory female flirt, as are the rehearsed and laconic deep tones of the male equivalent. The feelings of defeat and uselessness which can accompany old age are clearly discernable in the apathetic or querulous voice, sometimes exacerbated by the "tortoise" attitude, in which

An electronically generated voiceprint of a person saying the word "baby", displayed on a monitor screen. Such voiceprints reveal tiny differences even when the same person tries to repeat the same word. They show that every utterance is unique.

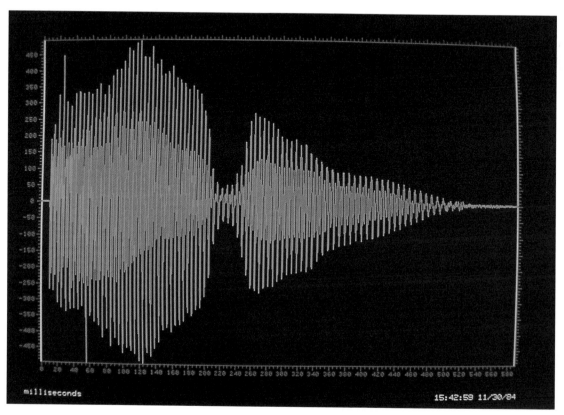

VOICE CHARACTERISTICS	LIKELY PROBLEMS
Lacklustre, descending pitch during phrases and sentences, narrowed tone lacking the highs and lows of expression	Exhaustion on every level, physical and mental
Sad-sounding, habitually "on the verge of tears" for no apparent cause	Imbalances related to the respiratory system, such as nasal, throat, or lung infections
Angry-sounding, for no apparent cause	Liver, gall-bladder, and spleen disorders
Fearful and anxious, trembling and hesitant	Bladder and urinary troubles
"Thickened" tone, with slow and drowsy articulation	Migraine, nausea
Exaggerated "sing-song" inflection	Preoccupation with the past, with fantasy, or feelings of superiority
Blocked or strangulated voice	Humiliation at work, loss of self-image, or silence enforced by others
Temporary voice loss	Shock, bereavement, sexual trauma, feelings of emotional imprisonment.
Stressed, forced voice with rapid, jerky speech, "explosive" consonants, over-emphatic delivery	Warning signs of circulatory disorders, high blood pressure, hyperactivity

the person withdraws the head into the neck—since the shoulders should always be below the jaw line for the voice to function naturally.

Integrating past, present, and future

Some health or lifestyle problems may be rooted in your experiences and relationships from the past, which you have not reasoned through or resolved; others may stem from your fears for the future. Such fears and anxieties about the past or future can upset your perception of the present, and disrupt your clear acknowledgement of the passing of time.

For instance, you may find yourself dwelling on an event that happened some months or years before. "Living in the past" like this is bound to affect the way you deal with the present. You may harbour guilt or feelings of remorse, that have not yet found their full outlet.

SINGING FOR TIME EXERCISE

Releasing the past Approach this exercise with an open heart, full of love, and a blameless, non-judgmental attitude to yourself and others. Choose an event in your life about which you feel vaguely uneasy or unsatisfied. It may have been an argument, a "white lie", or an untold secret. Go back into your memory and recreate the experience. Try to recapture the sensory impressions of the event: the sounds, sights, touches, tastes, and smells. Re-live how you felt, your thoughts and emotions. Strive for a "re-run" of the experience, but with new and open compassion.

Now, sing out loud—to your memory. Sing your thoughts and feelings. Sing what you would have done and said at the time, knowing what you know now. Appreciate that life experiences are your teachers, and that everyone else associated with the event was learning, too. Benefit from your mistakes. Also, understand that the mistakes should not remain monuments to error and regret, because when you recognize their educational meanings, they cease to exist. Conclude the exercise as described below.

Disarming the future You can "pre-live" projections of the future, in the same way that you re-live re-runs of the past. Proceed as described above, but select a likely test or duty that you will face, and which seems full of dread. Create an imaginative "video" of this challenge-to-be. Again, work from the anchorage of your open heart, full of love, and empty of critical judgements. Sing out loud for everyone who will play a part in the future events. Dedicate your words and your tune to the strength, wisdom, and love with which you can, and will, meet the situation. Singing through this "preview" of the event can allay your fears and articulate your worries, so that they may be rationalized.

Conclude these exercises by bringing your awareness and your love firmly back to the present.

Many people are helped by expressive movements to therapeutic sounds. In Eurythmy, gentle movements and postures are linked to certain vowels, consonants, and other speech sounds and vocalizations.

This fragmentation of your temporal awareness may contribute to dis-ease and suffering. You can use your mind and voice in simple exercises, as described on page 106, to bring your consciousness of time back into wholeness and harmony. Such a re-integration of past, present, and future is a vital part of the therapeutic process.

Singing is effective in such cases because it unites every level of consciousness and involves you as a whole person. This means residual doubts cannot lurk in dusty corners of

SINGING TO RELEASE PAIN EXERCISE

Pain, like a wrong note, is energy misplaced and imprisoned. This exercise helps you to identify, locate, communicate with, and ultimately release any pain you are feeling, replacing it with natural harmony. It is akin to re-tuning yourself, as you would re-tune a musical instrument. It may feel strange initially, as you try to "get to know" your pain, but you would not try to tune an instrument without first listening carefully to it, and identifying the wrong notes and other problems. Take about fifteen minutes to work through the activity, alone or with a friend as "questioner".

Relax Lie down in a position that minimizes stress and tension. Allow each part of your body to relax and "let go". Experience feelings of ease, warmth, and expansion. Give particular care to areas that seem tense and resistant.

Get in touch with the pain Ask yourself the following questions: When did the pain begin? When did I first notice it? Is it large and generalized, or small and sharply focused? Does it have a colour, a sound, a texture? Does it move? Is it hot or cold? Does it make me angry, afraid, or depressed?

Visualize your breathing Now that you know the pain, concentrate on your breathing and its rhythm. Visualize each in-breath as light entering your body and circulating to every part, filling each microscopic cell with new life and energy. Watch as the light surrounds and encapsulates the pain inside you with a luminous sphere.

Sing the pain away Now sing on each out-breath. Select the musical notes that have resonant links with the type or location of the pain, as detailed in the chart on page 90. Use the sound vibration to loosen the pain, in its bubble of iridescence. Visualize the pain lifting and floating, out and away from your body, still completely encapsulated in its light bubble. Keep concentrating on it and ensure that it disappears into the deep blue haze of the distance.

your mind, or manifest themselves physically as areas of body armouring (see page 73). Moreover, the true meaning of "repentance" is re-thinking events and situations, and getting your mistaken ideas back on course. Simple but effective singing exercises utilize your voice as the instrument of this therapeutic process. As the thinker of your thoughts, you can redirect them to heal your memories or your fears, however painful they may be.

Body parts and sound waves

Recent research by sound therapists and biologists has demonstrated the effects of sound vibrations on living cells. Using tuning forks as the sound source, the different frequencies of the musical scale caused blood cells to change colour and shape. For example, the note C made them longer, E made them spherical, and A changed their colour from red to pink. The frequencies of the notes may be sufficiently close to the cells' own natural frequencies to set up sympathetic vibrations, reinforcing resonances, and breaking up disruptive interference patterns.

Compared to healthy cells, cancerous cells can be thought of as weak, floppy, and overweight. Subjected to the same sequence of rising frequencies, they gradually became disrupted, and disintegrated at 400-480 Hz (A–B above middle C). It is possible that resonances strengthen healthy cells and tissues, and discourage unhealthy cells. This research may represent the beginnings of the therapeutic use of sounds for cancer treatment.

Similar phenomena, with healthy cells reinforced and unhealthy tissues discouraged, may underlie the effectiveness of tuning forks in sound therapy. The single-frequency pure tone of a tuning fork is unaffected by changes in temperature, and as instruments for sound healing, tuning forks have much to offer, being easily carried, resistant to wear and damage, and simple to use.

Tuning forks can be employed in a variety of ways in sound therapy; two techniques are described on page 111. If you become interested in their properties and effects, collect

as many as you can, beginning with middle C (256 Hz). Work up the notes of the scale, especially E, G, and A.

Using instruments

Some people feel naturally drawn to working with musical instruments, as described for the use of instruments in meditation (see page 96). When healing with sound, all manner of instruments can be brought into play, including the simplest of "toys", so that no one need feel excluded.

Percussion instruments such as home-made drums can help you to establish and strengthen the rhythmic patterns on which your body depends. Listen to or feel your own breathing or heartbeat, and set up your drumming to that tempo. Percussion instruments also provide an outlet for emotional release and expression. And they encourage the movement—physical, emotional, and mental—that enables you to recover or enhance your mobility, agility, and freedom. As you become immersed in the sounds and rhythms,

"Listening to music should bring out everything that is best in us. It should be like wind in our sails bringing our ship nearer to our heavenly predestination."

Peter Mikael Aïvanhov

Numerous household objects can be employed as percussion instruments. Make sure you have plenty of space and that the sounds will not disturb others, since it is difficult to concentrate if you feel uneasy.

TUNING FORK EXERCISES

These activities enable you to become familiar with the pure tones of tuning forks, their effects on body and mind, and their potential for healing.

Touch tuning Activate the tuning fork, preferably middle C (256 Hz), as described on page 18. Experience its vibrations by placing the stem of the vibrating fork on the palms of your hands, soles of your feet, and crown of your head. Lie down and ask a partner to hold the vibrating fork's stem at various sites along the centre of your chest and down the back of your spine. You will probably feel certain sensitive "trigger points", in the same way as the voice exercise on page 85. Likely trigger points are the atlas bone at the top of your spine, and the upper tip of your breastbone, just below the hollow of your throat. At these sites, the vibrational energies of the fork are resonating and harmonizing the energies of your cells, bones, muscles, and tissues.

Aura tuning Choose a tuning fork with a frequency that corresponds to the problem in question (see the chart on pages 90-91). Lie face down and proceed as above, but avoid direct contact with the fork. Ask your partner to hold the tuning fork between three and eight centimetres (one and three inches) from the surface of your body. In this way the fork will still be within your aura, the invisible energy field that surrounds your body. Your partner works down your spine, repeatedly activating the fork and holding it above your skin for each vertebra. At certain positions, it induces vibratory energies in your body, which may feed back to the fork and slightly modify its sound. Concentrate on these locations, and focus on the feelings of increased wellbeing, reduced pain, better emotional balance, and a positive state of mind. Conclude this exercise by "grounding" your energies. To do this, both you and your partner should centre your consciousness in the heart, and touch the Earth beneath your feet.

you can release deeply instinctive feelings and connect to your subconscious, replacing inertia and restriction by balance, equilibrium, and confidence.

Wind instruments, even a home-made bamboo flute or simple recorder, have a valuable role in the recovery of individuality. Compared to many other instruments, your sense

INSTRUMENTAL EXERCISE

Emotional conflicts are implicated in many problems, both physical and mental. This exercise can help to bring your unconscious thoughts and emotions to the surface, as a form of self-discovery; at this point the sounds can continue to work and assist healing. Use a small drum, or improvize one from a suitable object, with a playing surface about twenty-five centimetres (nine inches) across. Find a quiet setting, so that you can concentrate without disturbing others.

Begin very quietly. With the fingers of your left hand, gently tap out the rhythm of your own pulse. Keep this rhythm going. With your right hand, starting softly, make a short pattern of taps; then rest. Repeat the pattern, or tap a different one, slightly louder. Imagine that your right hand is telling the story of how you feel about yourself, with the drum as your voice. Let it speak for you. Build up the rhythms, making them as powerful and complex as you wish, all the time keeping the pulse rhythm with your left hand. The sounds gather to a crescendo, and your story is completely "told". But do not suddenly stop the music. Allow it to subside gradually, becoming quieter and more relaxed, until only your left-hand pulse remains. This continues in unison with your heart, for another few moments. Then relax, and all is quiet.

Recall your thoughts and feelings while the drum was "talking". What did it say about you that you did not know, or were not aware of? Did it ask questions about past events and conflicts? Now that these are out in the open, you can consider the best ways to deal with and resolve them.

Crystals of pure quartz (see page 114) are colourless. Tiny amounts of other minerals turn them beautifully translucent shades of green, brown, blue, yellow, and pink.

of timing and expression, and your own personality, come out in the notes you play with your own breath. The music assists you as you strive for a true sense of self, to find your own voice and language. Thus wind instruments are useful for overcoming problems rooted in fear, by encouraging your self-worth and sense of equality with others. They also help to deepen and improve your breathing.

String instruments, such as violins, require the most acute listening abilities. Playing a violin or cello, in particular, is based on your awareness of the ear-brain-finger feedback loop. It requires accurate placing of your fingers on the fingerboard, to make sure the notes are precisely in tune.

Playing a string instrument can assist in re-establishing and improving relationships in all areas of life, by establishing tuneful harmony. It is also an aid to resolving conflict and all forms of loneliness—including self-hatred.

Crystals

There has been a resurgence of interest in recent years in the properties and uses of crystals for many forms of therapy, including sound therapy.

There is a special relationship between the vibrational states of sound, and the rigid, geometric organization of molecules within a crystal. Sound is transmitted as moving molecules in gases and in liquids. But the molecules within a crystal—such as the billions of silicon dioxide molecules that make up a quartz crystal—are held tightly in a geometric lattice. Impinging sound waves or other vibrational phenomena compress and distort the whole crystalline structure. The result is the release of an electrical charge. The frequency of the incoming vibrations defines the frequency of the outgoing electrical charges, which can be detected as tiny bursts of electricity. This is the well-known piezoelectric effect, employed in many gadgets, such as old-fashioned crystal pick-ups on vinyl record turntables, telephone mouthpieces, and gas cooker lighters.

The reverse also applies. If fluctuating electrical energy is applied to a crystal, it releases mechanical energy in the form of vibrations, which can produce sound.

Crystals can therefore be regarded as transformers of energy. This is the basis of their role in healing and meditation: they focus and balance various energies. Crystalline deposits in the Earth are believed to balance the electromagnetic forces that are connected with ley lines. The human being has equivalent lines of force up and down the body, in the meridians of acupuncture, along which flows *Chi*, the vital energy. It is probable that crystals respond to sound energies, transforming their significant frequencies into the electromagnetic dimension (see page 23), and possibly intensifying and amplifying their energy content. The healthy

"Atoms are harmonic resonators."
Andrew Glazewski

MUSIC AND CRYSTAL ACTIVITIES

Simply holding a crystal, while listening or meditating to music, helps to heighten your sensitivity and deepen your insights. Test the freedom and vitality of your voice without a crystal, then with one held to one of the sensitive trigger or Chakra points (see page 118). There are no set rules here. Work from your heart, and trust your intuition. Meditate upon the qualities of strength, patience, self-forgiveness, peace, and the release of pain.

Listen inwardly for the "music" of therapeutic energy, for you are seeking to evoke and resonate its vibrations. Allow any sounds that you feel inside to manifest themselves through your voice; to be born into the physical world on the current of your breath. Sing these sounds into your crystal and envisage the sound waves being transformed into light. This light is focused and ultimately transmitted as a "carrier wave" of healing.

"The disciple should have a heart as pure as a crystal,
A mind as radiant as the Sun,
A soul as vast as the Universe,
And a spirit mighty as God,
and one with God."

Peter Delinov

electromagnetic balance of living cells is partially maintained by quartz (silicon dioxide), so by using this crystal, you can convert sound into healing energies and re-transmit them at the appropriate frequencies.

If you are interested in working with crystals, consult an experienced crystal therapist about their selection and maintenance. Choose them with loving care; although some would say that they choose you, via your intuition! Crystals are inorganic but never "dead". They should be dedicated, rested, and cleansed from time to time. Quartz is a good initial choice. Other suitable crystals include garnet, fluorite, rock salt, topaz, apatite, and beryl.

Specific healing frequencies

Sacred numbers, ratios, and musical intervals abound in ancient wisdom. Sometimes they are veiled in symbols, sometimes openly proclaimed. An example is the apparently innocuous number 432. Yet consider these connections. In

Hindu tradition, a day in the life of Brahman is the equivalent of 4,320,000,000 Earth years. Each of these days is divided into ages with the following ratios: 4:3:2:2. Our present age, the *Kali Yuga*, is held as the longest and most traumatic, and covers a period of 432,000 Earth years. In deep meditation, the human body's average breathing rate is 432 breaths per hour. And at an average rate of 72 beats per minute, the human heart beats 4,320 times in one hour. In music, these numbers represent the ratios of the musical intervals of the 4th, the 5th, and the octave (doubling or 2).

Scientific research has identified specific sound frequencies that relate to parts of the body. Therapeutic application of the appropriate frequencies can help disorders in those parts.

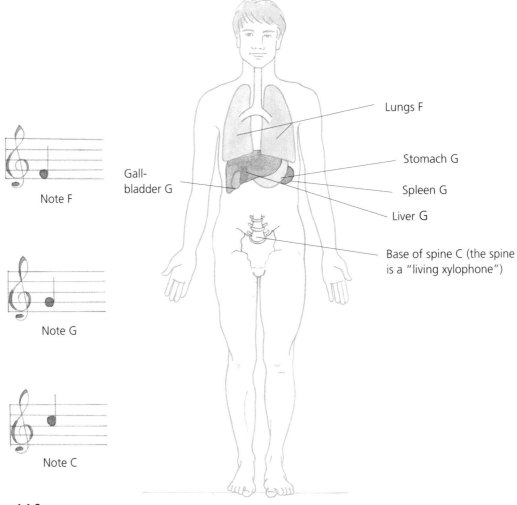

Note F

Note G

Note C

Lungs F

Stomach G

Gall-bladder G

Spleen G

Liver G

Base of spine C (the spine is a "living xylophone")

There are many similar examples. They reinforce the notion of the vibrational nature of creation, and provide the philosophical basis for many therapies: gem and flower essences, Bach flower remedies, homeopathic medicine, radionic and psionic medicine, dowsing, and numerous others. They are all concerned with the matching of resonant frequencies. Healing in the twenty-first century will undoubtedly make more use of light, colour, and sound, calibrated to the vibratory rates of chemical elements, cells, organs, organisms, and states of consciousness. Composers of healing music will employ the salient frequencies of audible sound, and the range of human voices, for curative and preventative applications.

How can you employ specific frequencies for therapeutic purposes? Researchers have identified certain frequencies that correspond to structures, organs, and functions in the human body, as shown on page 116. The key sound frequencies can come from tuning forks, the relevant notes on a musical instrument, musical compositions written in the key of these notes, or from your own voice as you hum, sing, or chant the notes, and the musical scales or compositions involving them.

In choosing appropriate sounds (see the chart on pages 90-91), be flexible to your own responses. Gradually you should gain enough experience to trust your developing intuition. Try to avoid a mechanistic approach, such as "ten minutes of humming F three times daily, to disperse gallstones". The open sensitivity required by all forms of holistic therapy is itself part of the healing process. In addition, there are many other significant frequencies beside the 12-note scale familiar to Western ears. These include Oriental scales and Indian *ragas*, which deserve exploration.

It must be emphasized that this area of investigation is in its infancy, and essentially experimental; no hard and fast conclusions should be drawn. However, doorways seem to be opening. Experimenting with vowel sounds and harmonics, for example, has been found to stimulate the brain and also the pituitary gland—the body's chief and controlling hormonal (endocrine) gland just under the brain, often referred to as the "leader of the endocrine orchestra".

The nasal cavity inside your nose is an important acoustic chamber in the vowel vocalization process, and classically trained singers have long regarded it as a target for the placing and resonating of certain vocalizations.

Indian mantra yoga teaches that there is a small energy centre or minor Chakra, the Bija Chakra or "centre of all sounds", that corresponds with this centre of vibrational activity. In the head, the roof of the mouth acts as a sounding board that transmits the vibrational energies through the

The seven chief Chakras, from the root of the spine to the crown of the head, are linked to various organs and systems in the body. Each Chakra has an associated musical note, and a mental-emotional "realm".

CHAKRA AND MUSICAL NOTE	SITE	BODY PARTS	REALMS
Crown B *Sahasrara*	Crown of head, top of skull	Upper skull, cerebral brain, right eye; pineal gland	Spiritual will and awareness, super consciousness
Brow A *Ajna*	Between eyebrows, above bridge of nose	Ears, nose, left eye, nervous system, skull base; pituitary gland	Intuition, perception, clairvoyance
Throat G *Vishudda*	Whole of throat area	Neck and voice, lungs and chest, mouth; thyroid and parathyroid glands	Self-expression, creativity, imagination
Heart F *Anahata*	Heart area, behind central breastbone	Heart and chest, circulation, lungs, arms, hands; thymus gland	Love, compassion, service to humanity
Solar plexus E *Manipura*	Base of breastbone (sternum)	Stomach, liver, diaphragm, gallbladder; spleen and pancreas glands	Personal emotions, desire, personal power
Reproductive D *Swadhisthana*	Between navel and groin	Pelvis, belly, sex organs, nervous system, low spine; adrenal glands, and sex glands (ovaries or testes)	Vitality, movement, sexuality, grounding
Root C *Muladhara*	Root or base of spine	Legs, feet, genitals, anus, base of spine, kidneys; the body's life force	Primordial origins, physical will to survive

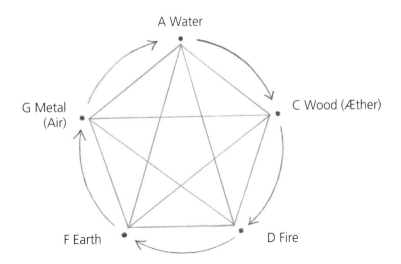

A Water

G Metal
(Air)

C Wood (Æther)

F Earth

D Fire

The geometric shape of the regular pentagon reflects the five-fold systems of Chinese medicine and the pentatonic (five-note) musical scale popular in ancient China. Each note is linked to one of the basic elements of earthly matter.

The symbol for yang and yin, indicating the perfect balance and constant interaction of energies in healthy existence. Diseases stem from imbalance.

oral and nasal cavities, via the Bija Chakra, and on to the higher mental and emotional centres in the brain.

Ancient theories on music and sound

From the earliest times, the function of music in Chinese culture was to reflect and maintain the harmonics of heaven and earth—the balance of energies, as exemplified by yang and yin (see page 30). A person's auditory pleasure, when hearing and perceiving the sounds, was of secondary consideration. Certain types of music had negative connotations. Sensual compositions were believed to threaten the stability of the ruling state, and loud music was despised as a cause of melancholy.

The foundation note of all music was the *Huang Chung* or "yellow bell", which had mystical value as a universal principle, like the Aum (see page 84). The *Huang Chung* was manifested in Earthly music by the division of the musical octave into 12 parts, known as *L'ius*. Although the *L'ius* were not used in the same way as our familiar musical scale today (see page 24), they provided the foundation notes for the twelve months and the twelve-year cycles of the ancient Chinese calendar. Seven-note scales were rarely used in China. The basis of composition and improvization was the five-note pentatonic scale (see also page 32). This scale has been termed the "Megalithic Scale", since it is found in the traditional music of ethnic cultures traceable to the Bronze

119

Age. It has also been prevalent in many parts of the world, from the Hebrides and Lapland, through Inuit communities of the far North, to South American Indian cultures, and more recently, in innumerable folk song melodies such as *Auld Lang Syne*. It reinforces the basis of music and all vibrational phenomena in the origins of humanity, which is in turn rooted in the planet itself, as another manifestation of the music of Gaia.

The easiest way to experience the five-note pentatonic scale is to play the black notes on the piano or keyboard. This is a wonderful way to be introduced to music, even for young children, because no matter which black notes are played—nor, indeed, how they are played—"mistakes" are virtually impossible. No painfully wrong notes exist in the pentatonic system.

In Ancient China, once the foundation note of the period was established, all instruments were tuned to this scale. The five-foldness of the musical philosophy is reflected in the complex pentagonal systems of Chinese medicine, as shown on page 119. In these systems, the hands and fingers are seen as being reflexed to the body's heart area. This is why keyboard or piano playing is regarded as good for the heart, both physically and figuratively.

Conclusions

Nothing in the cosmos stands still. The state of absolute zero temperature, minus 273.15°C, when all atomic vibrations cease, is admitted as unattainable by scientists. What is more, everything moves within a milieu of movements: cycles within cycles, wheels within wheels. Apparent immobility is a result of matched speeds. Thus every event influences every other event, with infinite implications.

Human consciousness presently roams between two vibratory parameters: the life-span of the universe, and the minutest vibration of an atom. The long-sought fulcrum or balance point is elusive, being hidden within the itinerant soul or spirit of ourselves. Beyond the physical body and the intellectual self-knowing mind, the most significant

"You can't pick a dandelion! A dandelion isn't a thing; it's a PERFORMANCE!"

Arthur Moor

120

therapeutic expansion is that of identity: "Who am I?" Living organisms exist within physically and biologically defined structures, but our human consciousness has no such boundaries. Enlightenment and healing are achieved by the extension of our vibratory spectrum, inward to our emotions and hearts, and out to the planet, Gaia, and ultimately to the cosmos.

Healing relies on an openness to the whole; a willingness to relinquish whatever frustrates or delays—mistaken ideas, negative feelings, poor diet, inadvisable lifestyle—and to accept a wider spectrum of responses with new ideas, experiences, and priorities. Healing is communication; and music, in its universal nature, is total communication. In the deepest mysteries of music are the inspirations, the pathways, and the healing which lead to one-ness and unity.

Deep in space, galaxies and star systems whirl on a cosmic scale. This is the ultimate realm of human consciousness, freed of physical and biological constraints.

USEFUL ADDRESSES

Many organizations and groups are discovering the value of sound therapy, so this list is certain to grow in the near future. In the first instance, write to the address shown. For local groups, contact your library or information bureau.

Association of Professional Music
Therapists in Great Britain
48 Lancaster Road, London N6
4TA
Publishers of the Quarterly Journal of Music Therapy

Jill Purce
Inner Sound and Voice Workshops
c/o Gillian McGregor, Garden Flat,
9 Yonge Park, London N4 3NU
Overtone chanting in Tibetan and Mongolian traditions

Fabien Maman
L'Alliaz, 1807, Bloway, Switzerland
Courses on healing with sound

New World Cassettes
Paradise Farm, Westhall,
Halesworth, Suffolk IP19 8BR
"New Age" recordings

Planet Tree Music
2 Thirlmere Road, Muswell Hill,
London N10 2DN
Original compositions, pealing music, Performances, shape tapes

Voice Work
Chloe Goodchild, 6 Goldney Road,
Clifton, Bristol BS8 4RB

Musicosophia Creative and
Therapeutic Listening
25 Hatch End, Forest Row, East
Sussex RH18 5DT

Healing Tapes
Ruth White and Trisha Lawriston
8b Hillside Gardens, London N6

Cymatics
Dr Peter Guy Manners
Bretforton Hall Clinic, Main Street,
Bretforton, Vale of Evesham,
Worcester WR11 7JH
0386 830537

Music/Healing Workshops
Pauline Wills, 9 Wyndale Avenue,
Kingsbury, London NW9 9PT

Earth Sounds
The Earth Centre, The Old Mill,
Skeeby, Richmond, North
Yorkshire

Ray Didcock
58 King Georges Avenue, Watford,
Herts WD1 7QD
Workshops on healing sound

Voice Workshops
Harriet Buchan, Salisbury Road,
Edinburgh EH16 5AB

The Nordoff Robbins Music
Therapy Centre
2 Lissenden Gardens, London NW5
1PP

Promethens School of Healing
Dr Carol Brierly MB ChB BSD
MAct, 152 Penistone Road, Shelley,
Huddersfield HD8 8JQ
Courses include sound healing and vibrational medicine

Hawkwood College
Painswick Old Road, Stroud, Glos
GL6 7QW
0453 764607
Courses on music, appreciation, performance and esoteric significance

Muz Murray
Inner Garden, 105 Gales Drive,
Three Bridges, Crawley, Sussex
RH10 1QD
Mantra and chanting, Yogic sound

Hygeia College
Theo Gimbel
Brooke House, Avening, Glos GL8
8NS
Courses on colour and music

Beautiful Painted Arrow
c/o Hannah, 41 Ashley Road,
London NW19 3AG
Esoteric Sound in Native American tradition

Judith Seeng
Esoteric Healing Sounds
Tel 081 450 2723

New Age Classics
18 Hopefield Avenue, London
NW6 6LH
Tapes of therapeutic Music including healing songs by John Saxby

Tomatis Therapy
The Marsden Centre, 30 Oliver
Lane, Marsden, Huddersfield HD7
6BZ

Pulsed Electro-magnetic Energy
Kay Kiernan
Bluestone Clinic, 16 Harley House,
Marylebone Road, London NW1
5HE

Jayne Chilkes
12a Vista Drive, Redbridge, Essex
IG4 5JE
Music therapy and original compositions

Cantillation Research Foundation
John Diamond and Peter Bloch
Tel 081 297 1976

Centre Chakra
Friedrich Glorian
La Roche Saint Secret, 26770,
Tanlignan, Drome, France
Research into music of Sacred Geometry and Platonic Solids

Mu Sum Ba Living Rhythm
Thomas Christen
4 Bramstone Road, London NW10
5TU
Rhythm and voice work to tune body and consciousness

Cycles of Nature
Jean Chapman
Queenswood, Topps Heath,
Bedworth CV12 0DP
Colour, Sound, Form, and Poetry for the Joy of Living

Raaha Soami Satsang Beas
Mrs W Whiston
2 Halepit Road, Great Bookham,
Leatherhead, Surrey, KT23 4BS
Specialized "Yoga of the Sound"

BIBLIOGRAPHY

This selection of books is designed to guide the reader into more specialized areas of sound and music therapy. Some titles are regularly updated or reissued, so consult your supplier for the most recent editions.

Jenny, Hans *Cymatics Vols I & II* Basilius Presse, A G Basel ISBN 3 85560 0090

Hodson, Geoffrey *Music Forms* Theosophical Publishing House, London ISBN 0 8356 7519

Marcotty, Thomas *The Way Music* Clear Calm & Co, Wellington, Telford, Salop UK

Gimbel, Theo *Form, Sound, Colour and Healing* C. W. Daniel & Co Ltd ISBN 0 85207 146 9

Halifax, Joan *Shamanistic Voices* Pelican Books ISBN 0 14 02 227 31

Blair, Lawrence *Rhythms of Vision* Destiny Books ISBN 0 89281 320 2

Lawdor, Robert *Sacred Geometry—Philosophy and Practice* Thames & Hudson ISBN 0 500 81030 3

Totton, Nick & Edmondson, E M *Reichian Growth Work* Prism Books (UK), Nature & Health (Aust) ISBN 1 85 327016 4

Stebbing, Lionel *Music and Healing* Krisha Press ISBN 0 87968 555 7

Jean, James *Science and Music* Cambrige University Press

Stewart, R J *Music, Power, Harmony* Blandford Books ISBN 0 7137 2121 9

Stewart, R J *Music and the Elemental Psyche* Aquavian Press ISBN 0 85030 444 6

Scott, Cyril *Music, Its Secret Influences Through the Ages* Gordon Pr ISBN 0 8490 0676 7

Hamel, Peter Michael *Through Music to the Self* Compton Press ISBN 0 900193 53 0

Govinda, Lama A *Foundations of Tibetan Mysticism* Weiser ISBN 0 87728 064 9 Chronica Botanica India ISBN 0 317 94161 5

Rooley, Anthony *Performance: revealing the orpheos within* Element Books ISBN 1 85230 160 0

Green and Gallwey *The Inner Game of Music* Doubleday (USA), Pan Books (UK) ISBN 0 330 300 17 2

Clynes, Manfred *Sentics: The touch of the Emotions*, Unity Press (Aust), Prism Press (UK) ISBN 1 85327 025 3

McClellan, Randall *The Healing Forces of Music* Amity House ISBN 0 916349 34 9

Tame, David *The Secret Power of Music* Destiny Books ISBN 0 89281 056 4

Beaulieu, John *Music and Sound in the Healing Arts* Station Hill Press ISBN 0 88268 057 9

Keyes, Laurel Elizabeth *Toning—The Creative Power of the Voice* De Vorss & Co ISBN 0 87516 176 6

Wilson, Thomas *Wind and Voice* Minim Books, Dublin ISBN 0 9509401 00

Spock, Marjorie *Eurythmy* Anthrosophic Press ISBN 910142 88 2

Stebbing, Lionel *Music Therapy—A New Anthology* New Knowledge Books, Fowler & Co

Leonard, George *The Silent Pulse*

Wildwood House Ltd ISBN 0 7045 0391

Campbell, Don G *The Roar of Silence* Quest Books, Theosophical Publishing House ISBN 0 8356 0645

Garfield, Laeh M *Sound Medicine* Celestial Arts ISBN 0 89087 483 2

Rudhyar, Dane *The Magic of Tone and the Art of Music* Shambhala ISBN 0 87773 220 5

Whone, Herbert *The Hidden Face of Music* Gollancz ISBN 0 575 01 739 2

Godwin, Joscelyn *The Mystery of the Seven Vowels* Phanes Press ISBN 0 9339999 86 0

Goldman, Jonathan *Healing Sounds: The Power of Harmonics* Element Books ISBN 1 85230 314 X

Berendt, Joachim Ernst *Nada Brahma: The World is Sound* East West Publications ISBN 0 85692 176 9

Berendt, Joachim Ernst *The Third Ear* Element Books ISBN 1 85230 049 3

Bentov, Itzhak *Stalking the Wild Pendulum* Destiny Books ISBN 0 89281 202 8

Orff, Gertrud *The Orff Music Therapy* Schott & Co (London) ISBN 0 901938 59 9

Priestley, Mary *Music Therapy in Action* 2nd ed. MMB Music ISBN 0 918812 32 1

Alvin, Juliette *Music Therapy for the Autistic Child* Oxford University Press 0 19 816276 6

Steiner, Rudolf *The Inner Nature of Music and the Experience of Tone*, Anthroposophic Press ISBN 0 88010 074 5

Werbeck, Sväarstöm *Uncovering the Voice* Rudolf Steiner Press
ISBN 0 85 440 570 4

Cain, Angela *The Voice Workbook* Headway, Hodder & Stoughton
ISBN 0 340 54215 2

Crowley, Brian and Esther *Words of Power* Foulsham & Co (UK), Llewellyn Publishing (US)
ISBN 0 87542 135 0

Huntley, H E *The Divine Proportion: A Study in Mathematical Beauty* Dover Publications Inc. (NY
ISBN 486 22254 3

Joudry, Patricia *Sound Therapy for the Walkman* Steel & Steele (Canada)
ISBN 0 9691687 0 5

Godwin, Joscelyn *Music, Mysticism and Magic* Penguin
ISBN 0 14 019040 6

Khan, Inayat *Music* Sufi Publishing

McClain, E G *The Myth of Invariance* Nicholas Hays
ISBN 0 89254 012 5

Hills, Christopher *Nuclear Evolution* University of the Tree
ISBN 0 916438 09 0

Halpern, Steven *Tuning the Human Instrument* Spectrum

Halpern, Steven and Louise *Savary Sound Health: Music and Sounds that make us Whole* Harper SF
ISBN 0 06 063671 81

Blofeld, John *Mantras, Sacred Words of Power* Mandala

Easwaran, Eknath *The Mantram Handbook* Routledge & Kegan Paul Ltd
ISBN 0 7100 8974 0

DISCOGRAPHY

This selection is based on the effects of sounds and music observed in therapeutic practice. Listening to sounds and music is an intensely personal experience, so use the list as a starting point for your own collections. Follow your intuition along any avenue of musical experience that you feel may be of benefit. Note that recording labels and catalogue numbers are constantly being updated. Consult your supplier for information.

The Harmonic Choir Hearing Solar Winds David Hykes, Docoro (Radio France) 4 558 607

Your Favourite Bird Songs BBC 2CM 511

String Quintet in C Major Schubert, EMI CFP 41, 44 80 4

Overtones in Old European Cathedrals: Senanque Michael Vetter, Wergo 1987, distributed by Impetus

Adagio in G minor Albinoni, Erato TU 70231, distributed by BMG Classics

Cello Concerto, Introduction and Allegro for Strings Elgar, HMV ASD 2906, Angel 37027

Canon in D Pachelbel, DDG

Polygram 3300 317
Sky-Sound Conishead: Midsummer Eve's Dream Obtainable from The Manjushri Institute, Centre for Buddhist Studies, Conishead Priory, Cumbria, UK

Music of Six Centuries Durham Cathedral Choir, HAC 832

Memories, Dreams, and Incantations John Saxby, obtainable from New Age Classics, 18 Hopefield Avenue, London NW6 6LH, UK

Hymn of Jesus Holst, Decca SXL 6006

Unaccompanied Violin Music Bach, Deutsche Grammaphon 3371 030

Unaccompanied Cello Music Bach, HMV SL S 798

Sequences and Hymns Hildegard von Bingen, Hyperion CDA 66039 7/85

Sacred Choral Works Palestrina-Allegri, Gimell CDGIM003 8/87, distributed by Gamut

Star Peace, Music of Tibetan Bowls Frank Perry, Mountain Bell 005, obtainable from The White Eagle Lodge, 9 St Mary Abbots Place, London W8 6LS, UK

Organ Music Toccata, Decca KCSP 583

Requiem Fauré, EMI Music For Pleasure, UB4 054
The Best of Vangelis Vangelis, RCA 25174, BMG Classics

"Barok Z" Bach and Handel, MC 198417, Teldec, distributed by Pinnacle
Jade Warrior—At Peace EASMI 120 µs, obtainable from Earth Centre, The Old Mill, Skeeby, Richmond, Yorkshire DL10 5EB, UK

Requiem in D Minor Mozart (K 6Z6), EMI Classics For Pleasure 4399

Sanskrit Chants, Ananda Ashram Cosmic Moments, obtainable from Inner Garden, 105 Gales Drive, Three Bridges, Crawley, Sussex RH10 1QD, UK

Introduction and Allegro: String Quartet Ravel, D 2733 007

Adagio for Strings Barber, Argo 2RG 845, distributed by Polygram

Violin Concerto No 1 Bruch, HMV ASD 2926

Kol Nidrei Bruch, DGG 2535 157

Fantasia on a Theme of Thomas Tallis and *The Lark Ascending* Vaughan Williams, Argo 2 RGC 15696, distributed by Polygram

INDEX

Bold type indicates main entry. *Italics* indicate illustrations and photographs.

ACKNOWLEDGEMENTS

The author would like to thank Eleanor, Ellen, and Steve at Gaia Books; Sir George Trevelyan for the Foreword; Pauline for her sisterly encouragement; and the many friends, teachers, and colleagues who have offered inspiration.

Gaia Books would like to thank Diana Bickley and Chloe Goodchild for their valuable comments and suggestions; Jane Parker for copy preparation; Philippa Underwood for proofreading; Christopher Nall for delivery services; Robert Denman and Chris Webb for meditational expertise; and Mary Warren for the Index

Photographic credits Clive Barda/Performing Arts Library pp. 36, 103: British Library (Ms. no. 21926: Tree of Jesse)/Robert Harding Picture Library p. 53: Celtic Picture Library p. 61: Eye Ubiquitous pp. 2, 19 (Frank Leather): Gaia Books p. 107 (Fausto Dorelli): Susan Griggs Agency p. 100 (Adam Woolfitt): Robert Harding Picture Library p. 83 (A. Evans): Hutchinson Library pp. 15 (John Ryle), 86 (Melanie Friend): Impact Photos p. 9 (Jeremy Nicholl): Magnum Photos p. 22 (Bruno Barbey): Ellen Moorcraft pp. 33, 110: Reflections p. 99 (Martin Dohrn): Science Photo Library pp. 10 (CNRI), 95 (NASA), 104 (Hank Morgan), 113 (Roberto de Gugliemo), p. 121: Janine Wiedel p. 66

BESTSELLING BOOKS FOR THE HEALTH OF BODY AND MIND
THE GAIA SERIES - FROM FIRESIDE BOOKS

FOODS FOR COMMON AILMENTS
by Dr. Penny Stanway
This concise guide gives advise on how to use everyday foods to prevent and treat 80 common health problems—from acne to migraine, and more.
0-671-68525-2, $10.95 ☐

MASSAGE FOR COMMON AILMENTS
by Sara Thomas
How to use the healing power of your hands to relieve everyday disorders—from asthma to menstrual discomfort, and more.
0-671-67552-4, $9.95 ☐

THE BOOK OF SHIATSU
by Paul Lundberg
The first detailed, step-by-step, guide to shiatsu—the ancient Oriental system of healing using hand pressure and gentle manipulation to enhance health and well-being.
0-671-74488-7, $14.95 ☐

THE NATURAL HOUSE BOOK
by David Pearson
foreword by Malcolm Wells
Combining home design with health and environmental concerns, this lavishly illustrated, comprehensive handbook shows you how to turn any house or apartment into a sanctuary for enhancing your well-being.
0-671-66635-5, $18.95 ☐

THE BOOK OF MASSAGE
by Lucy Lidell
From massage to shiatsu and reflexology, this book teaches you the power of the human touch.
0-671-54139-0, $13.95 ☐

THE WAY OF ENERGY
by Master Lam Kam Chuen
The first step-by-step guide to this unique and highly praised form of ancient Chinese medicine—motionless exercises that cleanse and strengthen your body and actually generate energy.
0-671-73645-0, $14.95 ☐

AROMATHERAPY FOR COMMON AILMENTS
by Shirley Price
This first-of-its-kind guide shows how to apply thirty of the most versatile essential oils to treat more than forty common health problems.
0-671-73134-3, $11.95 ☐

THE BOOK OF STRESS SURVIVAL
by Alex Kirsta
Learn to relax and stress-proof your lifestyle with this comprehensive reference on stress and management.
0-671-63026-1, $13.95 ☐

THE SENSUAL BODY
by Lucy Lidell
Reawaken your sensual self with this unique guide to mind-body exercises from around the world.
0-671-66034-9, $11.95 ☐

THE WAY OF HARMONY
by Howard Reid
A guide to self-knowledge and inner strength through the arts of T'ai Chi Chuan, Hsing I, Pa Kua, and Chi Kung.
0-671-66632-0, $12.95 ☐

ACUPRESSURE FOR COMMON AILMENTS
by Chris Jarmey and John Tindall
A step-by-step, instructional guide that demystifies this ancient healing art, teaching readers techniques to treat over 40 chronic and acute ailments.
0-671-73135-1, $11.95 ☐

THE TAO OF SEXUAL MASSAGE
by Stephen Russell and Jürgen Kolb
A step-by-step guide to the ancient Taoist system of sexual massage that will help you free your deepest and most joyful sensual energies.
0-671-78089-1, $15.00 ☐

YOGA FOR COMMON AILMENTS
by Dr. Robin Monro, Dr. Nagarathna and Dr. Nagendra
From cancer to the common cold—this holistic guide shows you how to use yoga to reduce inner tensions and heal the body naturally.
0-671-70528-8, $10.95 ☐

MAIL THIS COUPON TODAY - NO-RISK 14-DAY FREE TRIAL
Simon & Schuster
200 Old Tappan Road
Old Tappan, NJ 07675, Mail Order Dept.

Please send me copies of the above titles. (Indicate quantities in boxes.)
(If not completely satisfied, you may return for full refund within 14 days.)

☐ Save! Enclose full amount per copy with this coupon. Publisher pays postage and handling; or charge my credit card.
☐ Mastercard ☐ Visa
My credit card number is_____Card expires_____
Signature_____
Name_____
Address_____
City_____State_____Zip Code_____
or available at your local bookstore   Prices subject to change without notice